MEASURE, MIX & *Marinate*

Embracing the Key Ingredients to a More Fulfilling Life

CHERYL SCHUBERTH

Measure, Mix & Marinate: Embracing the Key Ingredients to a More Fulfilling Life
Published by Key Ingredients
Westminster, Colorado

ISBN: 978-1-7375895-0-1
SELF-HELP / Personal Growth / General

Cover and Interior design by Victoria Wolf,
wolfdesignandmarketing.com

*This book is dedicated to my sons, Jeremy and Colten.
Not only do they make me proud every day, but they inspire me
to continually grow and be deserving of their admiration.
They are the motivation for me wanting to empower more
women to level up and serve themselves and their
families at the highest level.*

CONTENTS

THE
APPETIZER

I'VE ALWAYS GONE AFTER WHAT I WANTED. I never felt anything was out of my reach. As a kid, I don't recall telling myself I wasn't good enough. If something intrigued me, I went after it. No second-guessing. No telling myself I couldn't because I was a girl. I didn't need to be the best. I was curious and wanted to learn in order to decide if it was for me or not.

I leaned towards being a tomboy and tried almost every sport available to me. By the time I was twelve, I'd played softball, soccer, basketball, tennis, racquetball, swimming, track, hiking, and was an equestrian. I'd added water polo, floor hockey, lacrosse, sand volleyball, and skiing by my college graduation. I was naturally athletic, but generally more drawn to the social aspect of sports than the performance aspect. *You look interesting. You play basketball. I'll try basketball.* Sports, for me, was more about connecting with people than winning.

I started playing soccer when I was five. Like many of my early interests, I played because my older brother played. After several years, I still wasn't aggressive and played only the minimum game time required, two quarters, although I showed skills in practice. My coach asked me if I didn't play well in games because my parents, who attended every game, made me nervous. I didn't have a good answer as to why I wasn't a better player, so I went with it.

When the coach suggested to my parents that they not attend my games, they were outraged. They told her they thought it was the stupidest thing they'd heard and kept attending every game. My parents never cared how good I was, but always wanted me to know they supported me.

A couple of years later, when we moved from Orange County to San Diego, I attended assessments for the soccer league. One of the coaches was impressed enough to pick me for his team in the first round. He talked about how excited he was for me to meet the other top players on the team. When we started practicing, I was embarrassed. I wasn't anywhere near the level of the other girls. However, because the coach had confidence in me, I stepped up. I started practicing and playing with all my heart. Because he believed in me, I wanted to be my best for him. While my skills were never on par with those top teammates, my progress made me realize I could do anything I set my mind to.

I tended to blend into a group and usually went with the flow. I had an opinion, but was happy to tag along with the crowd. In my earlier years, two individuals in my life thrived on making me feel like an outsider, like I wasn't worthy. I think this is why I tended not to assert myself too much. I didn't want to give them any more ammunition. As I became more physically distant from those individuals, I grew in my own direction and became more confident. This was about the time that soccer coach got a hold of me.

One experience can change everything, but we almost never recognize it in the moment. We often back away from challenges thrown at us when we're comfortable on the current path. We need to be intentional about whether to make the turn or stay the course. Make the decision to step up, or let the opportunity pass us by. Not accepting the challenge is a decision to stay where you are. The encouragement and belief from my coach drew me in. Choosing to push myself in response was pivotal.

Later on, as I gained more experience and navigated my career, I became a successful leader in technology. As the responsibilities of my corporate career grew, I struggled between the demands of my job and time with my family. I was driven to be my best, but I struggled to be the best mom and the best corporate go-getter at the same time. I felt the heat was always on high and my time at home was only about nagging the kids to complete chores and schoolwork. When we started getting into conversations with my oldest son about college, I realized we only had two years left with him, and I still had much to learn about my firstborn. This drove me to leave the corporate world. I had an opportunity to spend more time surrounded by positive, uplifting women in a new business venture, and a chance to help my husband get his start-up off the ground. Nothing was guaranteed, but I needed to make this change. I resigned from my corporate position and moved from the fast lane to the school zone.

When I was out of the corporate world, I had to learn to be productive without anyone setting boundaries for me. This happened about the same time the world began shutting down in response to a global pandemic and the school schedule changed to online-only, with no set hours. My focus became ensuring my teenage boys had enough structure to be productive and finding ways to support them and connect with them during the uncertainty. We embarked on a weekly, global culinary adventure where

I learned to let go. It was a way to enhance connection, be present, and make good memories during an awkward time.

As I wrestled with the drastic changes in my personal and professional life during this time, I reflected on what I had learned during my half century on this planet and what I would have appreciated understanding along the way. How the way that you measure your priorities, mix them in with your experiences and marinate on your understanding determines the direction of your life. But it all starts with the questions you ask yourself and others.

This book is a product of that time of reflection and a slower pace. An opportunity to connect with myself and my family with a deeper understanding of who we all are. I weave the results of our culinary experimentation together with my life experiences to, I hope, inspire you to become more inquisitive and take a hard look at where life has taken you and where you actually want to be. I will share how my focus on being my best and hitting my goals blocked me from confirming whether my goals were still serving me or those who depended on me. In my quest to be the best leader, mom, wife, and friend, I imposed my perspective and aspirations on others—instead of understanding how I could make the biggest difference for them. This put me in a place of controlling instead of enabling or empowering others, the role of a genuine leader and coach. Once I learned this secret, my career and my relationships unfolded.

In between each regional course, I've inserted palate cleansers as food for thought. In dining, the intent of a palate cleanser is to remove any flavor residue so that you can better experience the next course. I hope you stop and reflect on the scenarios presented to identify how you can optimize your experience in similar situations.

We all play an important role in our communities, our organizations, and in our families. Our journeys are unique, yet we are easily derailed by comparing our journey to someone else's. Everyone's path is unique and needs to be appreciated as such. While on our own course, we often neglect to look up from the path to understand if we are making the difference we want to make and if the path is still taking us where we are most needed. But none of that matters, if you aren't willing to take action.

In the past, I was always careful to put on a strong outer shell and conceal any vulnerability. This made it difficult for others to relate to me. I didn't appreciate failure as a critical component to success, and how by sharing my challenges, I could inspire others to start their journey. I'm here to share mine with you.

Your future starts with a single step. But first, you must decide you are worthy. Putting off the decision to start is deciding you aren't. There are people waiting to support you and be inspired by you, most of whom you have not yet met. They will reveal themselves on your journey. They are waiting for you to show up.

The world needs you. It needs to hear your voice. May this book inspire you to let the laughter and aromas pour from your kitchen as you embark on your own delicious adventures.

MAIN COURSE

POLISH

EVERY INCH OF KITCHEN COUNTER SPACE was in use. All five of us were busy measuring, stirring, rolling, sautéing, and baking. There was flour and oil everywhere. And most of us were wearing some of it. No one was thinking about clean-up, as we were simply trying to get the meal done so we could finally sit down and eat. It was after eight p.m., and we still had some work to do.

This was Polish night. One of the many theme dinners we endeavored to make as a family in an attempt to entertain and distract ourselves from the global pandemic. Jeremy, my oldest son, who was sixteen, was in the corner folding his blueberry mixture into dough for the sweet pierogies. He couldn't find the size tool the recipe called for to cut the dough and improvised. It may have resulted in more work, twenty-five pierogies instead of eight, but he was usually one to find a solution on his own, though not always the most elegant.

My mom was helping my husband, John, with the stuffed cabbage, chopping vegetables for the ground beef mixture. Mom is never one to sit and watch. She likes to be part of the action and is usually way ahead of us in the planning department. A few weeks into the dinners, she decided to take on the alcohol pairing instead of cooking since she didn't need to wait for us to do her part. We were a bit behind getting started on Polish night, and everyone chipped in where they could. Colten, my fourteen-year-old, and I were double-timing the potato and cheese perogies while John also prepared the kielbasa and peppers.

During the stay-at-home and safer-at-home orders of the pandemic, we organized thirteen theme dinners. We held our dinners on Fridays, as none of us had social plans during this time. All gatherings across the country had been canceled. The vision was to sample unfamiliar recipes and learn a little about each culture along the way. Everyone would contribute in the kitchen, but one person would pick the region for the week, compile recipes, make the grocery list and coordinate us all. This particular week, John was in charge of the meal. Shopping was a little erratic during the time of shut down as you were never sure what would be on the shelves when you went to the store. Because of this, my intention was to shop for each theme dinner at least the day before. This would give us time to adjust or try another store, if needed. I'm not a fan of scrambling at the last minute.

In normal times, John prefers to do the grocery shopping each week. I know, lucky me. It all started with me buying him a fancy cooking fork for our first Christmas together to encourage him to cook. I bought him the matching spoon the next year. At the time, I got home from work after six o'clock most nights. He was a trader at the Chicago Board Options Exchange and was done when the bell rang at 3:02 p.m. every day. Him picking up most of the cooking responsibilities allowed us to spend more time together in the evenings, and likely helped us get through the first couple of years of our marriage. Not having to cook after a long day working with demanding clients was significant for me.

Because John isn't much of a planner, knowing what we have in the house allows him to more easily pull a meal together. Completing the grocery shopping enables this. However, John more consistently shops by price, and I often don't consider price and buy what I want. I'm all about efficiency. I save time. He saves money. In reality, John doing the grocery shopping has mostly saved us from arguing. As a result, he has maintained the title of head shopper.

This week, shopping didn't actually start until four p.m. Friday evening, right after John pulled the recipes together. I let him do the shopping. By the time John returned from the store two hours later, he was the only one who had seen the recipes. None of us knew what we were supposed to be doing or prepared for the three hours of chopping, rolling, cooking, and baking in front of us.

Chaos is not my strong suit. I can make order from chaos, but need time to evaluate each thread in the ball of confusion. I'm all about assessment and thought into what's required. I pulled one all-nighter in college, and the stress of the disorder it caused overwhelmed me. I'm not sure I retained anything. You can imagine how being married to someone who doesn't plan and is distracted by every squirrel can be a challenge. I try to be flexible, but also know John can interrupt whatever I'm doing when he's geared up for the next conversation.

As a family, Polish night was definitely the farthest we'd ventured outside our comfort zone in the kitchen. It required a group effort to find recipes we could all agree on. When researching dishes and asking friends for suggestions, *Golumpki*, or stuffed cabbage, kept resurfacing. Ground beef inside purple cabbage? We were all skeptical. I hadn't eaten red meat in several years before we decided to undertake these culinary adventures, but the meal did not disappoint. Golumpki included.

The Unknown

While writing this book, I was trying to schedule a few hours to write without interruptions.

"Hey, honey. What do you have going on today?" I asked John.

"I don't know. I'm not a planner like you," he responded. I was used to these types of responses, but they still got to me. It was ten a.m. on a Saturday. I wasn't asking for his plans for the rest of the year, just the next few hours. I wanted to make sure we both got what we needed done, and he made me feel like I was crazy.

"I'm asking because I want to write for a few hours

uninterrupted, and I'm wondering if you're going to need my help in the yard."

"OK," he replied. "I'll get the boys to help if I need it for now."

My blood pressure went back down, and I didn't feel the need to strangle him anymore.

I mention this because I believe I'm better than most in appreciating differences in perspective. Understanding why someone thinks a certain way is incredibly helpful in avoiding unnecessary conflict and coming to the most productive solution. It often appears as if no one else's opinions matter. As if everyone, who doesn't believe the same as we do or approach life in the same way, is ignorant. Instead of listening and understanding why someone may have a certain viewpoint, we shut them down.

Each of us goes into a situation with our own lens. Our life experiences shape how we see, feel, and think about every scenario. None of us have identical experiences, yet we expect others to see, feel, and think the exact same as we do about a given situation.

I grew up in Southern California, and we ate a lot of Mexican food. There are a couple of taco shops I frequented in my teen years that I still stop by whenever I'm back in town. I met John after I moved to Chicago in my mid-twenties, and when we were dating, we went out to eat often. Trying to get my taco fix, I would suggest a Mexican restaurant every few times. We almost never went. I finally found out why.

"How about Uncle Julio's?" I asked.

"Nah. How about Italian?" he responded.

"Do you not like Mexican food? We never go," I retorted.

"Mexican food is what you eat at two a.m. after you've been out with your buddies," he responded.

Aha!

"What have you tried?" I inquired.

"Mostly burritos that made me feel awful the next day," he replied. He had only had greasy, late-night burritos that were "as big as your head" like the shop's slogan claimed. He had never had tasty, authentic Mexican food. Nor was I convinced the burritos were what made him feel awful, but that's how he saw it.

I knew where to start. If this relationship was going to last, tacos had to be in the picture. We started with homemade guacamole and chips. He was on board. Then we tried different Mexican restaurants. He slowly warmed up and now loves tacos almost as much as I do.

If I hadn't asked why he had that perspective, then I might have had a life of frustration without tacos or without John. It could have gone like this:

"What's wrong with you?"

"I just don't like Mexican food."

"Won't you even try?"

"I have, and it's not my thing."

It's a challenge to think clearly when we get frustrated, as when I was trying to get time to write or eat more tacos. I know these are simple examples, but I wanted to demonstrate two approaches. One is to ask why someone has a certain opinion or perspective and truly listen to understand. Not to respond. Don't be thinking about what you're going to say next but take the time to see their perspective. It doesn't mean you have to agree, but try to understand.

The second is to explain why you're asserting as you are. In my conversation with John about Saturday plans, it was clear I needed to give him more information to help him understand where I was coming from.

Polish night started out a little chaotic. None of us knew what we were making or what we were signing up for with the recipes we were given. When you're not a planner, delegating can also be a challenge. This is where the control freak in me came out, but I managed to keep it together. By looking through the recipes and asking specific questions, I was able to find out what John was feeling about the situation, what he wanted to make, and what he was comfortable farming out to someone else. We all pitched in where we could and had an amazing result. I think pierogies are going to make it into our recipe rotations going forward. There was some whining—I did mention the teenagers, but everyone was a good sport.

While the dinner preparation felt like it took forever, the food was incredible and worth the wait! The upside of dinner taking longer than expected to complete was spending more time, side by side, with my teenagers. For that, I would have eaten at midnight.

Stuffed Cabbage Rolls (Golumpki)

Yield: 1 dozen rolls

Submitted by Tyler Florence on foodnetwork.com

Ingredients

Sweet and Sour Tomato Sauce:

- 2 tablespoons extra-virgin olive oil
- 2 garlic cloves, smashed
- 1 1/2 quarts crushed tomatoes
- 2 tablespoons white wine vinegar
- 1 tablespoon sugar
- Kosher salt and freshly ground black pepper

Cabbage Rolls:

- 2 tablespoons extra-virgin olive oil
- 1 yellow onion, chopped
- 2 garlic cloves, minced
- 2 tablespoons tomato paste
- Splash dry red wine
- 2 tablespoons chopped fresh flat-leaf parsley
- 1 pound ground beef
- 1 pound ground pork
- 1 large egg
- 1 1/2 cups steamed white rice
- Kosher salt and freshly ground black pepper
- 2 large heads green cabbage, about 3 pounds each

Directions

Step 1 To make the sauce: Coat a 3-quart saucepan with the oil and place over medium heat. Add the garlic and sauté for 1 minute. Add the tomatoes and cook, occasionally stirring, for 5 minutes. Add the vinegar and sugar; simmer until the sauce thickens, about 5 minutes. Season with salt and pepper and remove from the heat.

Step 2 Place a skillet over medium heat and coat with 2 tablespoons of olive oil. Sauté the onion and garlic for about 5 minutes, until soft. Stir in the tomato paste, a splash of wine, parsley, and 1/2 cup of the prepared sauce from Step 1, mix to incorporate, and then take it off the heat. Combine the ground beef and pork in a large mixing bowl. Add the egg, the cooked rice, and the sauteed onion mixture. Toss the filling together with your hands to combine, season with a generous amount of salt and pepper.

Step 3 Bring a large pot of salted water to a boil. Remove the large, damaged outer leaves from the cabbages and set aside. Cut out the cores of the cabbages with a sharp knife and carefully pull off all the rest of the leaves, keeping them whole and as undamaged as possible (get rid of all the small leaves and use them for coleslaw or whatever). Blanch the cabbage leaves in the pot of boiling water for 5 minutes or until pliable. Run the leaves under cool water, then lay them out so you can assess just how many blankets you have to wrap up the filling. Carefully cut out the center vein from the leaves so they will be easier to roll up.

Step 4 Preheat the oven to 350 degrees F.

Step 5 Take the reserved big outer leaves and lay them on the bottom of a casserole pan, let part of the leaves hang out the sides of the pan. This insulation will prevent the cabbage rolls from burning on the bottom when baked. Use all the good-looking leaves to make the cabbage rolls. Put about 1/2 cup of the meat filling in the center of the cabbage, and starting at what was the stem-end, fold the sides in and roll up the cabbage to enclose the filling. Place the cabbage rolls side by side in rows, seam-side down, in a casserole pan.

Step 6 Pour the remaining sweet and sour tomato sauce over the cabbage rolls. Fold the hanging leaves over the top to enclose and keep the moisture in. Drizzle the top with the remaining 2 tablespoons of olive oil. Bake for 1 hour until the meat is cooked.

Step 7 Serve and pour any remaining sauce on top of each roll. I recommend you cut open each roll to cool before you enjoy.

Celery

When I was growing up, I recall someone calling me a jack-of-all-trades. I initially took it as a compliment (and it is), but when I heard the follow-on phrase, I felt defeated. Jack-of-all-trades, master of none. Did they mean I wasn't great at anything? I quit too soon, didn't work hard enough or apply focus? I remember looking for something to be great at, but could never find my passion. It turns out, my passion was being a know-it-all. Which is actually a jack-of-all-trades, depending on how you utilize and share the information. And by knowing just enough about the various areas of a given situation, I could direct the experts to create amazing things. My gift was getting people from various backgrounds to see eye to eye, embrace their differences, respect each other's talents and make magic.

One month into a position as a program manager, there were at least three different people sitting on my virtual couch telling me why they couldn't work with another individual on the team. I listened to each, heard their specific needs and concerns, and then went back to everyone with a new perspective. I understood enough about everyone's role and specific challenges to help each adjust their thinking and focus on what the team needed as a whole. The team reoriented to their new perspectives, and we delivered exactly what the client needed. Win-Win-Win.

I stepped into my technology career as a project manager in a digital development company. I typically got involved in a project after the customer had defined their work product and agreed on a cost with my company. Oftentimes, the customer initiator of the project was not involved in the day-to-day activities, and direction came from an intermediary responsible for executing. This is not uncommon, but can cause problems if the true outcome is not well understood by all parties. In one instance, we were contracted by a division of a major worldwide conglomerate to build a website. This was in the mid-1990s. The web was the new frontier.

The CEO of this conglomerate had told its businesses they had to have a web presence within ninety days. A little aggressive, but not completely unreasonable.

The challenge came when the intermediary decided they wanted all of their products available for searching and purchase in an online store. They were starting from zero. We tried to talk them out of it, but they wanted to go big.

Monday morning, two months into the project and after my team had worked all weekend, we had enough to show the client we weren't going to make it.

"Jim, you were supposed to have the product images to us last Wednesday so we could get everything sized for final testing. My team worked all weekend, and we are at risk for our Thursday deadline." This was my communication to our client's project lead.

"I know. I'm having trouble finding some of them, but you have to hold the Thursday target," Jim responded. "I have to deliver as committed!"

"We'll do what we can, but the team is burning out. We should look for another way this can be a success," I explained. The client was desperate. I could sense the culture he worked in wasn't accustomed to tolerating anything other than what the big man wanted.

As I brought the team together to look at options, we all agreed the original plan was not viable. Staying the course and not delivering would be worse than redefining the project. It took some convincing, but we worked with the client to rescope the work to deliver value we could stand behind and took it to the client's executive in charge. The executive thanked us for the transparency and agreed to support the new plan to his leadership team. But, he wouldn't tolerate another change. He was one of the executives being considered for the top position at the company and knew he needed to support the aggressive ninety-day plan which had been laid out by the incumbent. We delivered as committed, and everyone was pleased. That executive went on to become the new CEO for the corporation a few years later.

This project was a major win for me. Not because we completed everything the client originally wanted, but because we delivered a solid product the market was ready to consume. A product we could build upon to increase value over time.

Change is often viewed negatively, although change is constant. I understand the desire to follow through on commitments, but we are always learning as we go and should feel empowered to speak up and adjust direction based on what we learn. We usually don't have all the information when we start a project and should expect to find out more as we go. There shouldn't be a surprise when new details are discovered along the way. It's an opportunity for us to adjust.

Think about these situations:

- You're driving across the country and begin to see notifications about significant construction on the route.
    - Will a slightly longer way off the beaten path be more pleasurable than extended highway time in construction?
    - Will the two-lane frontage road be as crowded as the highway if everyone considers a detour?
    - Should we stay the course?

- It's obvious you won't meet your commitments to senior leadership.
    - Do you keep working the plan and cross your fingers the work comes together?
    - Should you blame the client for the failure and step away slowly?
    - Do you reevaluate and recommend a product website showcasing innovation and quality service in place of an online store for high-end medical equipment, when people are just now getting excited about buying books online?

- You've organized family activities to stay connected.
  - Do you control every element of the activities, ensuring it turns out exactly as you'd envisioned?
  - Do you start out slow and add structure as you go?
  - Do you enjoy the family time together given the confusing time of uncertainty, no matter what it looks like?

As we moved from one meal to the next, I let go of my initial expectations for the theme dinners and let them evolve. I see the original goal had no purpose other than as a starting point. The dinners morphed into memories greater than I could have ever created. And those thirteen weeks helped me transition from a corporate go-getter to a more open, vulnerable, and, I think, better version of me. But I'm not finished. We never are.

ITALIAN

FOUR WEEKS BEFORE POLISH NIGHT, John and I were in the mountains skiing for the week. The night before that we had been out on the town cheering on college basketball. March Madness was barely underway.

"Achoo," sneezed John. "I'm not sick!" he quickly shouted. The people around us chuckled. While the mysterious virus was causing whole nations to shut down, life in the United States was still mostly normal. There wasn't an empty seat in the sports bar. That quickly changed the next day.

The closures and cancelations were difficult to internalize, and we couldn't bring ourselves to get out to ski. And then March Madness was canceled. John handled it better than I thought he would. As an Indiana University alum and a Bobby Knight fan, March Madness is John's favorite time of year. We lounged around and watched a movie and then decided to go home a day early to be with our boys. This scenario was odd for us as adults, and I wanted to understand how they were feeling and be available for them.

The next day we learned spring break would be starting the following week, a week early. At the same time, we were mandated to shelter in place. It wasn't clear for how long or how deadly this virus truly was. The uncertainty was high, and information in flux. I considered us lucky, given we had a spacious home and all got along fairly well. A few days later, I learned the part-time coaching role I'd stepped into after I resigned was coming to an end. There was a lot of change being thrust on us all at the same time. My concern was how to leverage this time and not let it be a lost blip on the timeline.

That's when I had the grand idea of planning cultural theme dinners.

"So I was thinking, since we can't go anywhere, how about we plan theme dinners making food from a different country each week," I said. "Everyone can chip in and maybe we can look up some fun facts that go with the region."

This was my pitch to the kids. John was already on board.

"Suuurrrrre," Colten responded.

"Uh, OK," Jeremy added with a shrug.

"We could make some yummy food and then play a game or something," I added. Everyone bought in. There weren't many other options.

Between the five of us, we had varied cooking experience. John and I share the day-to-day cooking responsibilities, although he cooks more than I do. Colten taught himself how to bake and cook starting at age seven when he made his first pizza, including a crust from scratch, all by himself. Jeremy never showed a lot of interest in cooking and certainly nothing with more than three ingredients. Mom didn't cook much anymore but enjoyed helping out. She almost insisted on having a role in the dinners.

We typically ate a varied diet and rarely pulled our meals from a can or a box. Having had the opportunity to travel more than the rest of my family, I think I'm the most adventurous one of us and enjoy learning about the cultures I visit, as well. I'll try most local foods, though I do have my limits.

Baby Steps

For the first week, the boys picked Italy. I encouraged them to pick recipes we didn't already have in our regular rotation, but Italian was what they were comfortable with. Then they picked spaghetti and meatballs. I almost lost it. Didn't they understand my goal with this? The idea was to pick a completely new meal! But I went with it. We could still learn something together.

As we all took our assignments, we started to settle into this family time. Colten picked the recipes and started working on the meatballs. Jeremy was making the sauce. This was Jeremy's first experience cutting onions.

"Colten, do I cut them this way or that way?" Jeremy asked.

"It doesn't matter. Chop them up and put them in the pan

with the chopped garlic after the olive oil is heated. And don't let the garlic burn," Colten guided.

"How do I do that?"

"Keep stirring them and be ready to add the tomatoes when the onions are transparent," Colten responded.

"Got it." Jeremy followed Colten's directions, then popped his head up from staring at the pan. "What does transparent look like?"

They bantered back and forth, making jokes in between the instructional moments. It was sweet to see them working as a team. Being three years apart in school, they didn't have a lot of activities that overlapped. While they both played competitive soccer, they didn't play much together.

As any parent with more than one child can attest, their differences can be astounding. My kids included. Jeremy has always been a go-with-the-flow kind of kid, with Colten wanting to take charge. And Jeremy has never minded his younger brother wanting to lead. While Jeremy is a strong and confident kid, he often lets Colten do the heavy lifting. Intentional or not, I'm not sure.

In elementary school, whenever a fundraiser was rolled out, Colten was determined to win the biggest prize. It didn't matter how many people he had to talk to—he was in. When he was seven and Jeremy nine, Jeremy's Cub Scout pack had a popcorn fundraiser. Jeremy took Colten with him door to door to do all the talking. That cute little kid raked it in! His combination of courage and sweetness was hard to turn down. Colten's confidence and genuine interest in others have enabled him to impact many people.

Gutsy Move

When I was a student in Spain, I found myself talking with some new acquaintances in a small, empty bar. Translated from Spanish:

"Why do all of the Americans want to eat only American food while they're here?" one of my new friends asked.

"Well, I think we're all here for different reasons," I responded. "Many of them haven't traveled much and are getting used to being far from what they're used to. They're here for that first experience. I think familiar food is comforting and a reminder of those at home who miss them."

"What about you?" he asked. "You aren't worried about what you're going to eat."

I replied, "I came here because I love the Spanish language and want to be immersed in it to become fluent. The cultural aspects, including food, are a part of that. Also, growing up, I was never allowed to be a picky eater. My only option was whatever was served."

"Have you eaten blood sausage?" someone inquired.

"Yes, I have."

They were impressed.

At this point, the bartender pulled a plate with a large cube of what looked like Jell-O from the refrigerator. It was about the size of a cantaloupe, but squared off, and a deep red color. "Have you had this?" He took out a cheese slicer and carved off a sliver, offering it to me.

"What is it?" I asked.

"Are you sure you want to know before you try it?" the bartender responded.

"Yes, please," I countered.

"Pig's blood," he said, as he extended his hand with the slice further towards me.

I sat there for a few seconds, not sure what to do.

"Interesante, pero no, gracias," I responded. Congealed pig's blood was my limit.

Recalling our first theme dinner, while not adventurous, the time in the kitchen was relaxed, and the house smelled of an incredible Italian meal. We added Caesar salad, garlic bread, and gelato. It was simple, but it all came together nicely. Looking around the table, you could see the satisfaction on everyone's faces. Forks were clanking, sauce was blotted up with garlic bread, and food disappeared fast. Our playful dinner chatter, from the pride of making a meal together, carried into an entertaining family board game. The kids made sure I didn't win, but I forgave them the next day. The whole evening was filled with love, and pride, and laughter. And I had been annoyed with spaghetti and meatballs when this feeling was the real prize. How could I have wanted anything else?

Italian Meatballs

Yield: 8 servings
Submitted by Geanine on allrecipes.com
(slightly modified to use only beef)

Ingredients

- 2 pounds ground beef
- 2 cloves garlic, minced
- 2 eggs
- 1 cup freshly grated Romano cheese
- 1 1/2 tablespoons chopped Italian flat-leaf parsley
- salt and ground black pepper to taste
- 2 cups stale Italian bread, crumbled
- 1 1/2 cups lukewarm water
- 1 cup olive oil

Directions

Step 1 In a large bowl, combine beef, garlic, eggs, cheese, parsley, salt, and pepper.

Step 2 Blend breadcrumbs into meat mixture. Slowly add the water 1/2 cup at a time. The mixture should be very moist but still hold its shape if rolled into meatballs. Shape into meatballs.

Step 3 Heat olive oil in a large skillet. Fry meatballs in batches. When the meatball is very brown and slightly crisp, remove from the heat and drain on a paper towel. (If your mixture is too wet, cover the meatballs while they are cooking so that they hold their shape better.)

Step 4 Add to your sauce for the last 5 minutes of cooking to combine flavors. Serve over your favorite pasta.

Parsley

Early in my career, I was asked to lead a project team where the sponsors were in the United States and their constituent teams in Ireland, France, and Italy. We'd been asked to build a financing system to bring these three acquisitions into one tool. The team was going to Dublin to begin the analysis.

After introductions, the French team started to walk through the financing system they'd just completed. Our team was rightly confused.

I pulled the client sponsor to the side. "Troy, what are they doing? Don't they know we're building a whole new system? This one will no longer be needed."

He shook his head. "It doesn't sound like they know."

"No, it doesn't. Will you please tell them?" I pleaded. "We have a lot to cover this week."

Our first break lasted over an hour as Troy pulled the French team aside and broke the news. They were distraught and felt tricked. You could see it in their faces. They threatened to go back to France. After discussions with multiple layers of management in France and the US, we reconvened after lunch.

We all acknowledged the communication failure and our goal to move forward together, but there was still sensitivity around what had just happened. Our account manager, Debra from New

York, was direct in her style and as we continued, ignored the emotional situation. She neglected to realize the French team was working to build trust with all of us, including the sponsors from their own company. They were using the system they had recently built to connect the dots and move forward. Debra interrupted our team lead several times to redirect him as he tried to understand everyone's starting point and bring them all together. She made it difficult not only for the client navigating this challenging situation, but she was creating a rift within our own team. I had a better appreciation for the dynamic and took a stronger stance.

I began by asking questions to my team individually, four in addition to me, to understand everyone's perspective and get alignment on our goals.

How are you reading each of the client's team members?

Who are you concerned about?

What do you see as our biggest challenge?

What do you think we can get done with the rest of the time this week?

What do you need from the rest of our team and me?

What do you need from the client?

I asked similar questions of the client. As I gathered this information, I changed how I communicated with the team and our client to reflect this perspective and help the collective team move forward more cohesively. Debra was the outlier. She technically owned the client relationship, which, to her, meant she should be able to tell the team how to work. She was comfortable with me, but was not able to build rapport with the rest of the team as she did not seek perspective, but control. Considering how the week started, in the end we called it a huge success. We left Ireland with mutual respect across the two companies and a plan we could all work towards.

All teams go through stages of Forming, Norming, Storming, and Performing. Have you ever watched a new television series and struggled through the first few episodes, and then the characters clicked, and it was amazing? This is the acting team going through those phases. First, coming together and learning about each others' skills and styles and becoming their characters. Then landing on working norms and expectations. Third, pushing the boundaries on those norms and determining the best way forward, and finally Performing—leveraging the collective skills to make everyone their best. Trust is built as the team works through each stage. They will never get to the last stage if trust isn't established.

As the team progresses, maybe a character is re-worked, an actor switched out, a character minimized, or a new one added to optimize the troupe. But every time you make a change in team members, this process starts over as you've introduced new perspectives and new skills. Because of this, you must be intentional with change. Make sure you've asked enough questions to narrow in on the opportunity, and you don't take a good team down. Breaking up or adding someone new to a performing team can be as bad as having a missing ingredient. I can only imagine how challenging this was for *Game of Thrones,* where key characters were killed off every week!

Within two weeks of our return to the US, Debra was removed from the project, and I ran it solo. Not a situation I had seen at the company before or after. Later my manager praised me for the way I handled the "Debra-situation." I never saw it as handling her, but being able to read the dynamic and direct the team accordingly. Had I not asked questions, we never would have been able to accomplish our goals for the week or maintain a solid relationship with the client. Teamwork relies on everyone driving towards a collective, well-understood goal. It also requires trust amongst the team members. In my Debra-situation, instead of adding a new account manager, removing the current one and leaving everyone else intact allowed the team to move into the performing stage. And we did.

GERMAN

WHEN MY KIDS WERE FIVE AND THREE, my dad was diagnosed with Alzheimer's Disease. I immediately began researching ways to protect myself and my kids from a future with Alzheimer's and made significant changes to our diet. It wasn't seamless. There were battles, with my kids and my husband, but we landed in a reasonable place. On our journey, we noticed illness either didn't stop or typically didn't linger with us anymore. We were encouraged to keep going.

Earlier in the year of the pandemic, the boys had decided to try eating a vegetarian diet. We all jumped in together. We found some good meals, but struggled with lunches at school and finding decent choices when we went out to eat or traveled. After about two months—right before everything shut down—the boys grew tired of the challenges a vegetarian diet presented and decided to go back to the clean way we had been eating before, sort of.

For week two of our theme dinners, the boys decided they wanted hot dogs since they had been meat-deprived for two months. We had not kept hot dogs in the house for at least ten years. The one rule I had laid down for the theme dinners was no American food. The boys cleverly selected a German theme in order to eat bratwurst, the closest they could get to hot dogs. I was slightly annoyed with this selection, because they were working around my request, but given the uncertainty of everything going on, I wanted to give them whatever joy I could.

Jeremy signed up to make German potato salad. He questioned each ingredient as he added it.

"Do I cook the bacon first?"

"Yes, then crumble it up before adding it to the other ingredients," I responded.

After the bacon was done, and the potatoes cooked and sliced, he questioned again. "I have the potatoes. Now white vinegar? Do we have that? What does it look like?"

I pointed him to the bottom shelf in our pantry.

"Sugar? Normal sugar?" he inquired. I confirmed.

"Now add the bacon and onion?" he asked.

He'd never eaten German potato salad and had no context for the concoction.

After dinner, he commented, "I didn't think the potato salad was going to turn out too well." You could see the pleasure on his face as he ate his last bite. I think German potato salad is now on his list of favorites.

Colten was our dessert guy, more often than not. At an early age, he took to baking, and I remember being shocked when he made rolls from scratch when he was only nine. I had provided supervision, but he did everything else. He also started a pie bake-off tradition with my niece on Thanksgiving. The prize was a small plastic pie made on a 3D printer. In reality, we all won because the results were always impressive. This week Colten made the strudel, one of my favorites. I am always surprised by the raisins, but they work. Every time.

One of the things I was starting to appreciate with these theme dinners, especially as the kids were in a remote schooling situation, were the lessons. What do transparent onions look like? When to simmer versus boil? Should I stir or not stir? Why is it important to read ahead in the recipe? How and when to use the various utensils in a given situation? The boys were taking Home Economics and didn't even realize it.

Grow For It

As I leaned into being a better corporate leader, I started to realize the relationships and connection required to be the best for my team.

During the earlier part of my career, vulnerability had such a negative connotation for me. But I've learned vulnerability is required for courage and leads to connection. Connection breeds trust. Trust enables growth. Growth allows us to be more. More for ourselves. More for those who depend on us for nurturing and guidance. More for those who need to hear our story to be inspired to take their next step. More for those who can't help themselves.

There is a concept called *playing small*, popularized by spiritual philosopher Marianne Williamson. She stated: "Your playing small does not serve the world. There is nothing enlightened about shrinking so that other people won't feel insecure around you. We are all meant to shine, as children do."

Playing small refers to the desire to focus on short-term comfort and the validation it brings. It usually means we are giving up what we truly want to project a reality of acceptance and control. When we play small, our actions are usually motivated by insecurity, low self-worth, scarcity, and fear. Have you ever tried something new and were told it was a stupid idea, and you stopped? You chose to play small.

Playing big or small has nothing to do with the size of the accomplishment but the motivation behind your actions. If you are playing small, is it because you are afraid to make a mistake and prove the nay-sayers right or because you don't realize how much your story, your connection, your actions can make a difference for someone else? We usually become focused on what others will think if we do something new. We forget about who we can inspire by being bold and playing bigger *when* we do.

As I became more vulnerable and visible in my corporate life, I thrived. It felt good to be respected at the most senior levels of such a large company. But the saying is true: *The reward for good work is more work.* I took it on and spread it across my family time. I was incredibly responsive to every request, no matter the hour or day. Eventually, this began to negatively impact how I felt about myself as a mom. I'd spent many hours working to give my family a life of abundance, and I didn't have enough energy and compassion left to share with them.

I knew my understanding of the boys only scratched the surface, and now, as teenagers, they didn't voluntarily share. With Jeremy, a junior in high school, he wasn't going to be around for much longer. Jeremy is not the kind of kid you can understand by asking. You have to spend time with him and dig into his thinking in order to appreciate him. It can't be forced. With my work schedule and Jeremy's rigorous school and competitive sports schedules, casually connecting was a challenge. At the time, our conversations went like this:

"Hi, Jeremy. How was your day?"

"Good," he'd respond.

"What was good?" I'd probe, followed by a shoulder shrug from Jeremy.

"OK, so I saw you have a missing assignment," I'd state.

"I do?" Jeremy would retort.

"Yes. Check the tool," I'd say. "Are your chores done?"

"Sort of," was his response.

"So I guess that's a *no*? Make sure you get caught up."

"OK."

This conversation occurred almost every other day. Asking about Jeremy's family obligations was the only time I could engage him, with the exception of dinner, but those conversations were getting more difficult, as well. At dinner I would ask about the boys' *highs* and *lows* to pull out more details.

"What were your highs today?"

"We watched a movie in Science," Colten would say.

"What movie?" I'd ask.

"Something about rocks and earth. But we didn't have to do any work!" he'd respond.

This provoked some interesting discussion when they were in elementary and middle school, but they got tired of it as they got older.

"Not much different than yesterday," Jeremy would respond. "It's school."

Then after dinner, they'd retreat to their rooms, and I'd be off working again, whether in my corporate job or on another task I'd committed to.

I yearned for the connection I used to have with my boys and began to seriously consider leaving the corporate world. I knew teenagers naturally withdraw as they start to have their own interests and want more privacy, but I also knew I needed to be more present, mentally and physically. I gave my notice, and my long hours of full-time work turned into twenty hours of manageable effort in a less demanding role. When I finally did leave, I felt grief. While I'd made the decision to quit, I was leaving a world I had lived in for over twenty-five years. I sat with the grief for a few days and then embraced my new normal. I'd talked about leaving Corporate since Colten was a baby, but it wasn't the focus. Now it was reality.

This pivotal moment for my family and me was a decision to minimize regret. It's easy to put off decisions because we're comfortable and familiar with where we are. I had for over ten years. We don't realize by not making a decision, we're making a decision. We are deciding to stay. Deciding what we have or what we're doing is good enough. Be aware of the decisions you are making, and the impact not acting can have. The impact on you and on those around you. I heard from many people that they had been watching me and were impressed and inspired by my decision to make a change. A big change and not stay comfortable. I stopped playing small, and I inspired others to reevaluate their situation and decide if it was their time.

When you look at not taking a step as a decision, it changes everything. If you don't have a deadline or target identified as to when you are going to decide, then you've already made your decision. What you're doing now is good enough. We pretend we're still considering the option, but in fact we're afraid. We get more focused on what happens if it's the wrong decision instead of what happens if it's the right one. What if instead of falling, you fly?

The decision to try a vegetarian lifestyle had come up in conversation from time to time, but when the boys were ready, they went all-in and gave it their best. Ultimately, it proved more difficult than they'd hoped, but I was proud they had given it a shot. There's no harm in turning back, but you'll never know if raisins belong in strudel until you *decide* to give it a try.

German Potato Salad

Yield: 12 servings
Submitted by Tequila on allrecipes.com

Ingredients

- 9 medium (2 1/2" to 3" diameter) potatoes, peeled
- 6 slices bacon
- 3/4 cup chopped onions
- 2 tablespoons all-purpose flour
- 2 tablespoons white sugar
- 2 teaspoons salt
- 1/2 teaspoon celery seed
- 1/8 teaspoon ground black pepper
- 3/4 cup water
- 1/3 cup distilled white vinegar

Directions

Step 1 Bring a large pot of salted water to a boil. Add potatoes and cook until tender but still firm, about 30 minutes. Drain, cool, and slice thin.

Step 2 Place bacon in a large, deep skillet. Cook over medium-high heat until evenly brown. Drain, crumble, and set aside, reserving drippings.

Step 3 Sauté onions in bacon drippings until they are golden brown.

Step 4 In a small bowl, whisk together the flour, sugar, salt, celery seed, and pepper. Add to the sauteed onions and cook and stir until bubbly, then remove from heat. Stir in water and vinegar, then return to the stove and bring to a boil, stirring constantly. Boil and stir for one minute. Carefully stir bacon and sliced potatoes into the vinegar/water mixture, gently stirring until potatoes are heated through.

Step 5 Serve warm or at room temperature.

Peppermint

My brain thrives on making connections. Connections between other people but also connections between pieces of information. I questioned the way work was done, not to be difficult, but to understand the intention and optimize the outcome. As with the disconnect with the French team referenced earlier, by questioning, I was rewarded with a better perspective. The perspective of the author, the requestor, the end user, etc. This enabled me to better connect people within the organization and use the strengths of everyone I worked with more effectively. I became a Connector. There was no selfish reason other than wanting others to maximize their value and happiness in doing so. I connected friends this way. I connected coworkers this way. I tried connecting everyone where I thought there would be some value.

Because I became adept at asking questions, I also became proficient in reading people and their intentions fairly well. If someone's words and actions didn't match, then I minimized how much time I invested with them. I didn't want to get pulled into drama, and I wanted to spend my energy where it made the biggest difference.

In one role I held, I worked with a team of highly skilled technologists. They were constantly traveling and worked long hours to meet commitments to our customers and internal teams.

You could always count on them. I had a great experience with everyone I worked with until Chad was assigned to my project. He missed several commitments to the team, and when I probed, I got excuses and vague commitments. Not totally out of line, but the conversations felt off. Answers to my questions were non-specific, and I had little confidence in them. He had good skills, but he wasn't serving the team. I asked for someone new to be assigned to our project, and we executed as committed. A few weeks later, I learned Chad had been fired because he was using his company credit card to hide an affair. His loyalty wasn't to the company. Had I accepted his excuses, the team would have suffered. By digging in, I was able to get a better sense we were in trouble based on what he wasn't telling me.

Don't always take information at face value. If you can't connect the dots, then ask more questions. Don't let people who know more about a topic intimidate you into accepting their answers.

Of course, you have to read the individual to understand where and how to probe, but information, or lack thereof, is powerful. Also, don't confuse *questions* with *accusations*. With clarifying questions, you are asking to understand. The goal is for people you interact with to feel valued, not scrutinized. Ask questions as if you were a naive four-year-old, not a detective. It also helps to acknowledge you are the one with the knowledge gap. I've found this works both in communication with teenagers with an attitude and coworkers who have the full picture in their heads and assume you do, as well.

For example, "Tell me more about that. I understood the dependencies a little differently."

Instead of: "What are you talking about? You told me that step C was required, especially if you weren't going to do step B."

Or this one:

Fourteen-year-old son: Can I not do the dishes tonight? I have to finish a project in Science.

Mom: I thought you finished that over the weekend? That's why you were able to meet up with your friends.

Son: I finished what I had planned to do, and now I have to get caught up on math also.

Mom: Why are you behind in math? And now you want me to do your chores? I work all day and need you to contribute around the house, too.

Son: I know! Can you just get off my back?! I have a lot of work to do.

Or this alternate ending:

Mom: It sounds like there might be a prioritization challenge here. What do you think?

Son: I don't know. Maybe. I'm getting tons of homework, though.

Mom: I'll do the dishes tonight if we can sit down and talk about prioritization tomorrow. OK?

Son: OK. Thanks, Mom.

Another good way to diffuse a challenging situation and let people know you support them is to ask, "What do you need to be successful? How can I or the other team/family members help?" Focusing on the end game and not pointing fingers always produces better results. When people know you care, they are more willing to open up and focus on what's important.

I have used this approach countless times to get to clear agreements that enable the individual or the group to move forward. It also keeps everyone from churning. The expert still gets to be the expert, but we also get clarity and action.

WEST AFRICAN

ONE OF MY FAVORITE CLASS MEMORIES from college was when my African Literature teacher invited his students over to his house for lunch. I was a freshman, and he'd invited his upper and lower division classes over for an authentic West African meal. I remember running into a friend who I didn't know was in his other class, but otherwise, I only remember peanut chicken. It was amazing! I stuffed myself, and the food coma was worth it.

As we navigated which region to make dinner from next, I kept lobbying for an African country. The first three weeks were familiar—Italian, German, and Chinese, followed by Jewish for Passover. Everyone finally relented for week five. I was excited to show them how incredible peanut chicken was, and I was intrigued by what other foods we would find. Instead of one country, we chose West Africa. We made peanut chicken with rice, fried spinach, and lime cake. All new dishes for us.

As you might expect from a long ago memory, the peanut chicken wasn't as incredible as I remember, but it was still good. At least I thought so. The rest of the group wasn't ready for it. Peanut chicken is a rich stew, and the texture is varied. Peanuts, not crushed, mixed in with veggies and chunks of chicken. No one tossed any out, but over the next few days, I was the only one who ate the leftovers. I was disappointed, but decided the peanut chicken was too far out of my family's comfort zone. Too much, too soon. The lime cake was somewhat familiar and great with my coffee the next morning.

That Wasn't the Plan

I've never been one to shy away from a new idea. I'm usually open to anything as long as it doesn't go against my values or hurt anyone. I find it thrilling. I heard a quote from Neale Donald Walsch several years ago that captures the feeling perfectly. *Life begins at the end of your comfort zone.* I know not everyone can relate, but pushing myself keeps me going.

I grew up in the San Diego area. Spanish-speaking people and businesses were a part of my environment. I enjoyed the language and studied Spanish in high school and then abroad in Spain during my junior year of college. I adored the Spanish culture and language so much, six months after graduating college, I moved to Spain to live. A roommate from college lived in Madrid with her boyfriend, but I didn't know anyone else, and I didn't have a job. My goal was to land a corporate position where I could meet more people, improve my Spanish and start to feel like I belonged there.

I stayed with my former roommate for a couple of weeks until I found a room living with three other girls. They were all in their mid-twenties. The Spanish one—la Española—owned the apartment. My other roommates were from Peru and Colombia. This combination meant we all spoke with different dialects and accents. I didn't interact with them much initially. I was still getting used to being immersed in the language. Having lived in Spain previously for a semester abroad helped, but this time it was all Spanish, all the time. The varying word usage and pronunciations added to the challenge. It took me a few weeks to be able to understand someone on the first try, consistently. There was still significant vocabulary I needed to learn, but that was one of the reasons I was there.

It turned out Spain was in a major recession at the time I was there. Unemployment was close to 25 percent. As a new college grad, my skills weren't unique enough to get a work visa that would take a job away from a Spanish citizen. Instead, I taught English to businessmen on an hourly basis. I had three students totaling approximately eight hours of work a week. This actually gave me enough income to live on, but I wasn't meeting anyone new. I spent my free time exploring Madrid and trying to figure out where to meet more people my age, while staying safe. Not being 100 percent communicative in the language put me at risk of wandering into some place I didn't belong.

Given all of my work time was in English, and I was solo a lot of the time, I wasn't improving my Spanish. I went to the movies, watched TV (Erkle, from the TV show *Family Matters,* is much less annoying in Spanish than in English!) and anything I could to try to improve my Spanish or at least enjoy my time there. My college friend did include me in some outings, but she didn't have many friends outside of her boyfriend's group and their respective girlfriends. Breaking into a group with a language barrier was a little tough.

After only four months in Madrid, I decided to move back home. I was disappointed in myself. I didn't have the job I'd hoped for, many new friends, and I was lonely. A couple of weeks before I left, my roommate from Colombia, Luz Mari, invited me and our Peruvian roommate, Eliana, out with her and her fiancé, Javier. We went wine tasting and then the next day went out to his parents' ranch to relax and enjoy a good meal. We had smiles the whole time, and I was finally starting to connect with people. About a week later, Javier told me they were opening a Spanish/American restaurant, and he wanted me to help run it. He asked me to stay in Madrid and not go back to the US. I was surprised and flattered, but the idea was so foreign that I barely gave it any thought. I had already told everyone I was coming home and me running a restaurant was far from where I wanted my life to go. Although, I honestly wasn't sure where that was yet.

I went out to dinner with Javier and Luz Mari a week later.

I used an excuse to turn them down. "Thank you for the offer, Javier, but I already told my family and friends I'm coming home."

"Are you sure? We've narrowed down the locations and should start laying out the restaurant in a few weeks," Javier responded.

"I'm sure." I quickly changed the subject. "What are you going to name the restaurant?"

"We don't have a name yet," he retorted.

"How about Tía Molly's? Casual Spanish American," I suggested.

"We're not calling it Tía Molly's." And that was that.

The idea of running a restaurant in Spain was my peanut chicken. A little beyond what I was comfortable with. I came up with a lot of excuses why I couldn't and didn't consider why maybe I should.

African Chicken Peanut Stew

Yield: 8 servings

Submitted by Hank Shaw on simplyrecipes.com

Use chicken legs, thighs, or wings for this recipe. They have more flavor and will hold up better with the other flavors of the stew than breast meat. Also, browning the chicken pieces and cooking the stew with the chicken on the bone adds flavor.

Ingredients

- 2–3 pounds chicken legs, thighs and/or wings
- 3 Tbsp vegetable oil
- 1 large yellow or white onion, sliced
- A 3-inch piece of ginger, peeled and minced
- 6–8 garlic cloves, chopped roughly
- 2–3 pounds sweet potatoes, peeled and cut into chunks
- 1 15-ounce can of crushed tomatoes
- 1 quart chicken stock
- 1 cup peanut butter
- 1 cup roasted peanuts
- 1 Tbsp ground coriander
- 1 teaspoon cayenne or to taste
- Salt and black pepper
- 1/4 to 1/2 cup of chopped cilantro

Directions

Step 1 Heat the vegetable oil in a large soup pot set over medium-high heat. Salt the chicken pieces well, pat them dry, and brown them in the oil. Don't crowd the pot, so do this in batches. Set the chicken pieces aside as they brown.

Step 2 Sauté the onions in the oil for 3–4 minutes, stirring often and scraping any browned bits off the bottom of the pot. Add the ginger and garlic and sauté for another 1–2 minutes, then add the sweet potatoes and stir well to combine.

Step 3 Add the chicken broth, crushed tomatoes, peanut butter, peanuts, coriander, and cayenne and stir well to combine. Add the chicken. Bring to a simmer and taste for salt, adding more if needed. Cover the pot and simmer gently for 90 minutes (check after an hour), or until the chicken meat easily falls off the bone, and the sweet potatoes are tender.

Step 4 Remove bones and chop the cooked chicken. Remove the chicken pieces and set them in a bowl, until cool enough to touch. Remove and discard the skin if you want, or chop it and put it back into the pot. Shred the meat off the bones and put the meat back in the pot. Note: You can serve it with the chicken on the bones, but it is a bit messy, hence the recommendation to remove the meat and skin and discard the bones after cooking and before eating.

Step 5 Adjust the seasonings for salt and cayenne, then add as much black pepper as you think you can stand—the stew should be peppery. Stir in the cilantro and serve by itself or with simple steamed rice. We have varying tolerances for heat, so we kept the cayenne and black pepper to a minimum.

Step 6 Spoon into bowls over rice or plain and serve.

Pickled Ginger

In my twenties, I saw your career as defining who you are. An indicator of how much respect you deserved. I didn't appreciate how each role in our society and economy was important (with exceptions for illegal activity), and everyone's contribution deserves equal respect. As I started working with more executives, my appreciation grew.

One time I needed to complete a mundane task of printing, collating, and organizing materials for an upcoming meeting, which I expected to take several hours. I was dreading the task and still had a lot of work to do to be ready for the event. I asked around, and someone suggested I ask one of the executive admins to help. I was relieved.

I emailed an individual I did not know with the request and a short timeline. I don't think I asked if she had the time or would be willing to help, but sent the whole job over to her. Not surprisingly, she rejected me. I was annoyed. As the person running the product release, wasn't my time more valuable?

I had a hierarchical view of value and respect. For someone who was trying to climb the corporate ladder but still on the lower rungs, I think there was a little power play going on also. As I worked more closely with the administrative assistants in my organization, I began to recognize how invaluable those assistants are to any business. Experts in organization and coordination keep the executives out of the weeds and allow them to focus on the more critical needs of the business.

The more I appreciated them, the more they enabled me. By getting to know them and what they needed to be successful, I was able to make a bigger impact. I respected their abilities to get things done, and they were happy to help me. This thinking applies to every job.

As a rule, jobs exist because they add value to the organization or community. It doesn't matter if the role is as a janitor or CEO. They all bring value and deserve respect. Imagine if the office you worked in or a community organization you frequented didn't have someone cleaning it regularly. How would the disorder and uncleanliness impact the productivity of the people who worked there or the value of the services? We are all a cog in the wheel and deserve to be greased.

When Colten was four, I picked him up from daycare one night shortly before closing time. His classroom was in the back of the building and required us to walk down the long hallway to leave.

"Good night, Ms. Murray." He waved as we walked by her classroom.

Ms. Murray looked up and responded, "Good night, Colten."

"Good night, Brandon," he said, waving to a younger classmate.

Brandon ran over and waved both hands broadly in Colten's face, "Good-bye, Colten!"

"Good night, Joey," Colten shouted as he waved to the janitor. Joey looked up with a surprised expression on his face. He had no idea who this kid was.

I loved this child's view of worthiness and acknowledgment that we are all in this together. Colten has always seen beyond anyone's age, role, color, and skill and treated them with respect. It is one of my favorite things about him, and I hope he can not only maintain that view but share it with the world.

Thinking back to Spain and the offer to run a restaurant at twenty-four years old, I think it was simply too far out there for me. I knew nothing about restaurants. I had never worked in one and definitely didn't know enough Spanish to feel comfortable working with employees, vendors, or customers. I didn't know Luz Mari and Javier well enough to know how this would go, and I didn't want them to see I wasn't good enough or I wasn't who they thought I was. I felt my direction was more corporate/office, not hospitality and service, but that was likely an ego issue. I didn't want to get my hands dirty for a living. I overlooked this as my opportunity to become fluent in Spanish and meet more people.

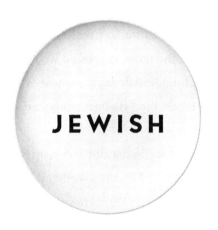

JEWISH

FOR THE FIRST FEW WEEKS of the stay-at-home order in the US, you never knew what you would find at the grocery store. For some reason, toilet paper was always in short supply, and grocery shelves were often bare. I remember one encounter with a store worker where I was looking for spaghetti and staring at an entire section of empty shelves at least twenty-five feet long. He asked if he could help me find something. There was an awkward silence as I glanced back and forth down the empty shelves. It was as if I was the only one who saw the emptiness. He was doing his job and trying to be helpful, but it felt like a scene from a horror movie.

Now imagine you're making food you've never cooked before. You're not sure what many of the ingredients look like—does it come in a box or a jar, is it large or small, and you have no idea where it would normally be in the store. And because of the virus, you're trying to minimize your contact with everyone and everything and spend as little time in the store as possible. Because it was Passover week, my mom suggested we make a Jewish meal. She used to work for a Jewish doctor whose wife would bring in various cultural foods, but I had never cooked a Jewish dish nor shopped for one.

I went to the store with a list and ended up going up and down almost every aisle before I finally asked and found out the store didn't have matzo crackers. We were making matzah ball soup, and the crackers were a critical ingredient. Additionally, they didn't have the right chicken parts for the soup—legs and thighs. Instead, I bought chicken breasts. Fortunately, we were able to locate the crackers at another store. I hoped cooking would be less stressful than shopping.

Mom, although in charge this week, asked me for direction regarding the various parts of the meal. I remember my mom as a decent cook in the kitchen. Her spaghetti sauce and lasagna were my favorites, but Hamburger Helper also had a regular spot on the menu. She was leading our Jewish meal, and I was surprised when she deferred to me for advice. I'm not sure if it was because she hadn't cooked as much recently or was afraid of the recovering control freak in the house, but it caught me off-guard.

"Cheryl, when do you think we should start the soup? What about the bread?" she inquired.

I hadn't read through the recipes and couldn't actually say, but also, didn't want to take over her meal. As I'd been learning to build up others and let go of control, I used questions to redirect ownership.

I refrained from taking the recipes and coming up with the start times. "Does anything need time to marinate or to cool?"

"Umm, no," she responded, reading through each recipe.

"How long does the soup take to make?"

"One and a half hours," she said.

"What about the kugel?"

"A little over two hours."

I went through all the items in the plan. "Is there a logical pause point where we can line up completion of the dishes to have them ready at the same time?"

This allowed her to talk through it and come up with relative starting times for each part of the meal. However, since she likes to be busy and not wait, she started the matzo ball soup early in the day and put the final touches on before we ate. Asking questions allowed her to realize what was possible and still own the process.

I had never made bread from scratch when I volunteered to make the challah and followed the recipe exactly as written. I even consulted our resident baking expert, Colten, to make sure I was understanding the directions correctly. Making challah was more time-consuming than I'd expected, but I don't think it could have turned out better for a rookie. I don't eat a lot of bread, but I definitely ate more than my share of the loaf.

Kugel was an interesting experience for all of us. There are several versions, but ours was a slightly sweet, egg noodle, pudding-like casserole. Essentially, a few versions of dairy, a couple of different sugars, cinnamon, vanilla, egg noodles, and raisins. Jeremy took this on because there were no onions. He was learning the challenges of cutting onions, and somehow got the dish with the most onions every week. This week he specifically asked for a dish without any onions. Given the unfamiliar combination, his approach was almost a repeat of German potato salad. The ingredients didn't sound right, but he kept going, confirming as he went.

Are You Sure?

Perspective is a result of each of our unique experiences. The collection of those experiences forms how we think, feel, and react to new situations. Those individualized responses can lead to arguments, frustration, and gossip if we don't check them. We assume intent based on what we know and what we have experienced, but we often have no idea what's actually going on with someone else. This is why I've always stayed away from the rumor mill. Assuming, or worse, making up reasons for someone's actions or inaction, can be hurtful and damage relationships. Before you assert on someone else's behalf, make sure you have the facts. I tend to be the pin to the gossip balloon. Fortunately, this means little gossip and the related drama come my way anymore.

"Did you hear Sheila and Jim were talking intently at the party last night?"

"No. Is everything OK?"

"I think so. I heard she gave him a big hug and kissed him on the cheek when they parted. Maybe they're getting back together."

"I know his mom was recently diagnosed with cancer. I think she was close with her. Maybe she was consoling him."

"I don't know. It sounded more intimate than that."

"Well, maybe we should check on her."

According to the University of Louisville Ekstrom Library, an assumption is *an unexamined belief: what we think without realizing we think it.* And they can be dangerous if not validated.

I never take a situation at face value when someone comes to me with a "What should I do?" situation. I've already talked about asking questions as a tool to help pull out information. I use them frequently to understand context and assumptions. Sometimes this irks people, like John, but he's gotten used to it. I've realized I don't have the same perspective as the person coming to me for advice or sharing an opinion on a situation with me. I try to see the situation from his or her seat. Why is this important to him? What assumptions is she working from? How did he get A + B = C? Giving advice or stating what I would do without understanding the full context might be worse than not providing input at all. Questions are powerful.

People may come to you for guidance because they respect your opinion or because they want an *Amen*-er, someone who agrees with whatever they say, but your opinion or input may be skewed if you don't have all the information. We can give guidance from our lens, but you also need to see through theirs. (Sometimes it's OK to be an *Amen*-er, but make sure you know the implications.)

One of my employees, James, was struggling to get the

information he needed to effectively manage and communicate on one of his programs.

"Cheryl, Ahmad is not showing up to the team meetings, and his responses to my emails are vague. I don't think he's on track, but he's afraid to tell me. I'm planning to talk with his manager, George, and ask him to replace Amhad on the team. What do you think?"

"Why do you think he's not on track?" I asked.

"He's avoiding me. I'm not getting any information," James responded.

"When's the last time you got any information from him?" I inquired.

"He hasn't been to a team meeting for three weeks. I reached out to him before the meeting this week to make sure he was coming. He didn't respond until after the meeting, and he didn't show up!" James was clearly frustrated.

"Have you talked with any of his peers on his team to see if there is anything they can tell you? Maybe there is something going on within their organization?"

"No," James stated.

"You know Sarah, right? Try asking her. If you don't get anywhere, then I suggest you reach out to George, but I wouldn't go in asking for Amhad to be replaced, but try to get more information," I coached.

"Are you saying I should try to get the status information from George?" James questioned.

"I would ask if there is another priority blocking Ahmad from engaging," I suggested. "Telling a manager their employee isn't performing can be a tough conversation and could put George on the defensive. Give George a chance to evaluate the scenario by considering your questions. Maybe Ahmad has had a family emergency. Also, I do know IT is integrating the systems from the two companies [we were several months post-merger]. There could be an issue with the data."

Assumptions can be dangerous, but we generally need to start somewhere. We compile thoughts or assumptions based on our lens. It's important to validate them before we go too far down the path they are leading us. Otherwise, we can get into trouble. Before you think the worst, gather more information.

As we dug into our Jewish meal, you could hear the silverware clanking. The sweet pudding noodles of kugel were a departure from our typical dinner in texture and flavor. Matzo balls looked like meatballs, but definitely had their own taste and feel. Although good, the soup wasn't as flavorful as expected. As we talked through why, we decided it was lacking salt because we had used a substitute cut of meat due to availability in the store. Adding salt to the leftovers made all the difference.

With this meal being new to us, we all had our own assumptions about how everything would turn out. But having done our own research, we can now speak to the flavors from experience.

Kugel

Yield: 16 servings

Submitted by minichef on allrecipes.com

Ingredients

Noodles

- 1 (12 ounce) package of wide egg noodles
- 6 large eggs, beaten
- 1 (16 ounce) package of small curd cottage cheese
- 2 cups whole milk
- 1 cup sour cream
- 1 cup white sugar
- 6 tablespoons butter, melted
- 1 (4 ounce) package cream cheese, softened
- 1 tablespoon vanilla extract
- 1 teaspoon salt

Topping

- 1/3 cup white sugar
- 1/4 cup brown sugar
- 1 teaspoon ground cinnamon

Directions

Step 1 Preheat oven to 350 degrees F.

Step 2 Grease a 9x13-inch baking dish.

Step 3 Bring a large pot of lightly salted water to a boil. Cook egg noodles in the boiling water, occasionally stirring until cooked through but firm to the bite, about 5 minutes. Drain.

Step 4 Beat eggs, cottage cheese, milk, sour cream, 1 cup white sugar, butter, cream cheese, vanilla extract, and salt in a large bowl.

Step 5 Stir egg noodles into cottage cheese mixture, then pour into prepared baking dish.

Step 6 Combine 1/3 cup white sugar, brown sugar, and cinnamon in a small bowl; sprinkle mixture atop noodle kugel.

Step 7 Bake in the preheated oven until sauce is bubbly and noodles are golden, about 1 hour. Allow the pan of kugel to cool on a wire rack for 10 minutes before serving.

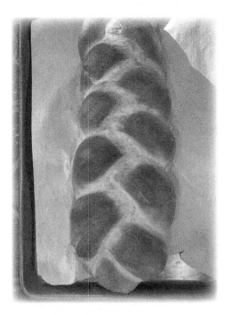

Tart Apple

A couple of months into the pandemic, as the country was trying to resume normal activities, we encouraged Jeremy to get a job. Since remote learning and a canceled soccer season kept him home most of the time, we wanted him to interact with more people and put him in situations where he needed to learn more responsibility.

"Jeremy, why are you against getting a job?" I asked.

"I don't spend much, and I don't need the money," he responded. He had never asked for much from us.

"I understand, but this isn't only about making money," I replied. "It's about taking direction from someone other than me or Dad and learning responsibility."

"But I don't want to fold shirts or make tacos," he pleaded. "I just want to program." He is a computer guy and planned to study electrical engineering in college.

I could hear the pain in his voice. He had always been focused on one friend at a time. He chose to limit where he spent his energy. I could tell having to meet new people who he might not otherwise pick, and spend hours with them, was what he was most against.

"Tell me why this is so upsetting to you," I pressed.

"It's not what I want to do," he urged emphatically.

"I understand, but is there something you're afraid of? A job teaches you many skills you will need to use when the position is more important to you," I reinforced.

"I can learn those when I need to," he replied.

Most new things Jeremy tried came easily. By asking questions, I learned he saw spending time learning skills outside his core competency as unnecessary. He would figure those skills out when the job was important enough to him. The questions also helped me educate him on the importance of learning when there is little to lose. We need exposure and experience to build muscle memory. We should not expect to be perfect when we start something new, whether it's a career, a new hobby, or being a parent. And we shouldn't beat ourselves up for not being as good as someone with more experience.

We need to give ourselves more grace. When I started practicing yoga, I was curious why the word "practice" is always used. We don't talk about practicing weight lifting or practicing writing. But life is continual practice. Repetition builds skill. As a mom, I'm always practicing. Practicing my patience, my problem solving, and my responsibility. I know I'm not the only one who was petrified the day I left the hospital with my firstborn. Other than a little babysitting and reading up on babies, I had virtually zero practice as a mom. And I am learning every day. I wasn't scared when I came home with Colten because I'd had some practice with Jeremy. But they are always showing me I have more to learn about being a parent.

No one ever claims to have mastered life. It's a constant process of learning and growing. The unexplored is what makes life interesting. Step into the challenges. They are the biggest goldmine for growth.

ARGENTINA

AS WE RESEARCHED RECIPES for Argentina night, we learned much of the food has roots in other regions as a result of several waves of European immigration. They also eat a lot of steak. While I'm not much of a steak eater, Argentina night was a delightful surprise. I initially had trouble finding the called-for flank steak, but after trying a few stores, I found exactly enough. It was surprising how after ten weeks into the great quarantine of 2020, the stores were still having trouble keeping the shelves stocked.

While the kids were excited for the steak, I insisted there always be a vegetable component. The vegetables turned out well, I made them, but I think the reason everyone gobbled them up was the smothering of chimichurri. Chimichurri sauce makes almost anything taste amazing.

While all the food was fantastic, the dessert stole the show. Colten and I tag teamed.

"What's for dessert, Colten?" I asked.

"I was thinking flan," he responded.

"Hhhmmm." I considered. "What other options did you come up with? I think of Mexico or the Philippines when I think of flan."

We went back to our phones to research.

"How about dulce de leche," Colten suggested.

"OK . . . How would we serve it?" I questioned. "What if we make sandwich cookies filled with dulce de leche? That would be tasty!"

As the master baker, Colten made the alfajores cookies, and I made a complete mess of the stove with dulce de leche everywhere. It was a dream. The treats melted in our mouths. I only wish we had made more.

My mouth watered over everything we ate that night. Chimichurri steak, roasted veggies with chimichurri sauce and empanadas, which we realized were a lot like pierogies, and dulce de leche sandwich cookies. And this non-steak eater had seconds of everything. The Malbec Mom contributed was the icing on the cookies.

Discovery

As noted, the culinary influences in Argentina are a result of the mass movement of Europeans into the area. While I haven't moved as part of a broader cultural shift, I have moved more than

twenty times in my life, but about eight times where I needed to make new friends. As a young kid, I always made friends easily. Our family went camping with most of our free time, and every camping trip, I wound up with a new buddy to spend my days with. I found new friends at my brother's soccer or baseball games and always wanted to bring them home with me. I was crazy shy around grown-ups, including close family friends, but could become best friends with another kid my age in a matter of minutes. But a group of kids was another situation.

I assumed by knowing one person in a group, everyone else would accept me. I didn't appreciate how shared experiences, good and bad, are what make relationships. You had to go have an experience together to earn trust and build deeper connections. You couldn't just meet someone, like the same TV show, and be BFFs. The experiences didn't need to be monumental, but meaningful. Like gravy or chimichurri spread across your entire plate. Each element of the meal is connected by the shared component.

As I noted previously, there were two different people in my extended circle who made me feel unworthy starting about the age of six. Whenever they were around, I always felt inferior. At the time, it felt like I was always having to prove I was better than they portrayed me, but I always felt defeated. When I was exposed to a new group of kids, I would try hard to prove myself to them. I would try to show them how great I was without having any real reason why they should trust me or follow my lead. I hadn't yet learned being trusted requires experience, and being a leader is about people being inspired to

follow you. Not about you taking control. Although sometimes timing is everything.

When my family moved from Orange County to San Diego, I was in fifth grade. I was nervous because it was in April, with less than two months left in school, and I was afraid I wouldn't have enough time to make friends before the summer. When I showed up on my first day, I felt like the shiniest object around. No one knew anything about me yet, but everyone was curious. I wasn't used to attention. The two "bullies" were no longer in my same city, but it took me a few days to embrace the new faces. However, it didn't take long for me to figure out who I had hobbies in common with, and I quickly developed a group of friends.

I wasn't doing anything intentional to attract people, but my newness was intriguing. I can't say I was the leader of my new group of friends, but I finally felt like I belonged. I could start being myself, and making new friends became more natural. No one was threatened by me and I attracted more people I could relate to. I drew in people and groups of various backgrounds, skills, and goals. This spawned increasing confidence and drove me to push my boundaries.

This was about the time I'd started taking horseback-riding lessons and started entering horse shows. I put myself out there for everyone to see. When you show horses, there are categories where the horse is judged and categories where the rider is the focus. Initially, the horse received all the glory, but as I continued to ride and my confidence on the horse increased, I started to get recognized also. I ran for class president in eighth grade. I didn't win,

but in the process, I met a lot of people who came from different elementary schools, and I gained more confidence just by expanding my circle. As I kept pushing myself, I realized you don't always have to hit your goal for your effort to be worth it. They say *aim for the moon, and you'll reach the stars.* Growth occurs regardless of where you end up, as long as you start. In my early years, I never had a lot of blue ribbons, but I did have a ton of experiences.

Being the one who wasn't afraid to dive into the unknown, I was often asked to take charge when a new challenge came up, or maybe I would volunteer for it. This role required me to solicit other people to help based on their skills and interest. And, as was required much later in my corporate career, being a good leader requires you structure or guide the group, the team (or the recipe) to allow each to complement and enhance the others. You wouldn't want a baseball team full of players with only catcher skills. If some could also pitch or play second base, you would leverage that expertise where you could.

One of the things I was able to do, after leaving my full-time corporate role, was to get more involved at the boys' school. I volunteered to work on the After Prom decorating committee. In case you aren't aware, the After Prom is an event held after the prom, 11 p.m. to 2 a.m., with food and activities to provide a safe place for the kids to go after the dance. They can only enter once. If they leave, to get alcohol for example, they can't come back in. The intention is to keep the kids out of trouble as much as possible.

Like most committees at the school, the After Prom committee took whoever they could get. The individual responsible for leading each subcommittee had no control over who volunteered and needed to figure out how to use the skills of everyone who showed up regardless of expertise. Our committee had a core of four people. I was the only one who didn't know anyone else. The others had been volunteering at the school for years. As the one who usually coordinates and drives projects, it was a nice change to let someone else take charge. Our leader, Susana, knew what the others could contribute, but had to get to know me and how I worked. As we worked through the plan and started building, she called on our individual expertise to focus on different areas of the project.

"Rachel is very creative. Are you OK if Rachel makes the monkeys?" Susana asked.

"Sure. I can cut them out once she has them ready," I responded.

"Great! You'd talked about the ticket booth. What are you thinking? Do you want to design that?"

"OK. I found some ideas on Pinterest. How much space do we have? I'm not as familiar with the layout,"

"Let's get some time in the gym to measure all of the spaces."

"Perfect." Susan understood what I needed.

From our exchanges, Susana learned I'm a detail-oriented, data-driven person. Measurements were important! And Rachel was more creative and was happy jumping into the work. And since our fourth member had participated in enough committees and driven several events for the school, Susana plugged her in wherever she was needed each week. She was an amazing resource. We ended up with an incredible team and completed a lot of significant decorations quicker than we'd expected. High-performing teams don't magically happen. They are guided. Guided by the team members themselves sometimes, but always by someone who can see how the individual parts will fit together best.

As reinforced in the story with Debra earlier, often one component of the team or recipe can make a significant difference in how it performs. We also experienced that in our Argentinian meal. We savored how the chimichurri brought all the flavors together to make it spectacular. None of the flavors in the meal were suppressed, but each were enhanced by the shared connection.

Alfajores

Yield: 12 cookies

Dulce de Leche

Recipe courtesy of Alton Brown as
featured on Foodnetwork.com

Ingredients

- 1 quart whole milk
- 12 ounces sugar, approximately 1 1/2 cups
- 1 vanilla bean, split and seeds scraped
- 1/2 teaspoon baking soda

Directions

Step 1 Combine the milk, sugar, vanilla bean and seeds in a large, 4-quart saucepan and place over medium heat. Bring to a simmer, stirring occasionally, until the sugar has dissolved.

Step 2 Once the sugar has dissolved, add the baking soda and stir to combine. Reduce the heat to low and cook uncovered at a bare simmer. Stir occasionally, but do not re-incorporate the foam that appears on the top of the mixture. Continue to cook for 1 hour.

Step 3 Remove the vanilla bean after 1 hour and continue to cook uncovered until the mixture is a dark caramel color and has reduced to about 1 cup, approximately 1 1/2 to 2 hours. Strain the mixture through a fine mesh strainer. Store in the refrigerator in a sealed container for up to a month.

Sandwich cookies

Recipe by Christine Gallary as published on Chowhound.

Ingredients

- 1 cup cornstarch
- 3/4 cup all-purpose flour, plus more as needed
- 1 teaspoon baking powder
- 1/2 teaspoon baking soda
- 1/4 teaspoon fine salt
- 8 tablespoons unsalted butter (1 stick), at room temperature
- 1/3 cup granulated sugar
- 2 large egg yolks
- 1 tablespoon pisco or brandy
- 1/2 teaspoon vanilla extract
- 1 cup dulce de leche, at room temperature
- Powdered sugar, for dusting

Directions

Step 1 Place the cornstarch, measured flour, baking powder, baking soda, and salt in a medium bowl and whisk briefly to combine; set aside.

Step 2 Place the butter and sugar in the bowl of a stand mixer fitted with a paddle attachment. Mix on medium speed, stopping the mixer to scrape down the sides of the bowl once with a rubber spatula, until the mixture is light in color and fluffy, about 3 minutes. Add the egg yolks, pisco or brandy, and vanilla and mix until incorporated, about 30 seconds. Stop the mixer and scrape down the sides of the bowl. On low speed, gradually add the reserved flour mixture and mix until just incorporated with no visible white pockets, about 30 seconds.

Step 3 Turn the dough out onto a piece of plastic wrap, shape it into a smooth disk, and wrap it tightly. Place in the refrigerator until firm, at least 1 hour.

Step 4 Preheat the oven to 350°F and arrange a rack in the middle. Line 2 baking sheets with parchment paper and set aside.

Step 5 Remove the dough from the refrigerator, unwrap it, and place it on a lightly floured work surface. Lightly flour the top of the dough. Roll to 1/4-inch thickness (the dough will crack but can be easily patched back together). Stamp out 24 rounds using a plain or fluted 2-inch round cutter, rerolling the dough as necessary until all of it is gone.

Step 6 Place the cookies on the prepared baking sheets, 12 per sheet and at least 1/2 inch apart. Bake 1 sheet at a time until the cookies are firm and pale golden on the bottom, about 12 to 14 minutes. (The cookies will remain pale on top.) Transfer to a wire rack to cool completely.

Step 7 Flip half of the cookies upside down and gently spread about 2 teaspoons of the dulce de leche on each. Place a second cookie on top and gently press to create a sandwich. Dust generously with powdered sugar before serving.

Cucumber

At most American universities, freshmen generally live in the dorms and navigate the newness of being an adult as a group. Hundreds of young learners packed into a building dealing with being away from family for an extended period of time, missing home, eating whatever and whenever they wanted; staying up as late and sleeping as much as they desired; learning you had to set your own boundaries in order to meet your educational goals for the semester.

When I went to college, instead of living in the dorms, I requested to live in the on-campus apartments. I felt I was sophisticated enough to skip the horsing around of the dorms and jumped ahead. There were few freshmen in the apartments, and I didn't appreciate that I would be missing out on lifelong connections many people have from enduring their freshman year together. Instead, I experienced my firsts with people who already had their firsts behind them. I made some good friends in school, but always felt like a bit of an outsider, as those friends had incredible connections from their freshman year.

Later in life, as I began climbing the corporate ladder, I thought my progress would be measured solely on my abilities to make and meet commitments. I glossed over the connections required for people to trust in you. As I talked earlier about my experience with administrative assistants, the thinking extended to all my coworkers and team members. As I focused on producing as an individual, I neglected the people. The people who relied on me to deliver trust and help them grow. I was always trying to skip ahead in the journey, and I often had to backtrack to get results.

After a particular round of organizational restructuring, I decided it was time for me to be more intentional about how I led my team. I was always proud of my organization and how we operated, but I felt we could bring more value, and I knew it started with me. I asked my human resources business partner to execute a New Team Assimilation exercise. This involved sharing information from our personal lives with each other and being open to feedback from my team about what they needed from me. This was a little touchy-feely for my comfort, but I wanted to be better for those who looked to me for leadership.

I don't know if my team knew how uncomfortable I was with the personal discussions, but I did my best to be open and genuine. Initially, the more candid conversations felt forced, but I consumed everything with an open mind and began being more open and real.

As I sent an email with a photo from a recent vacation and the caption "Guess where this was?" I felt silly, bordering on ridiculous. My intention was to share a personal experience, but it felt a bit like bragging. Most of them played along. I shared photos several times, and then the personal conversations became more common in our team discussions and in my individual conversations with each of my direct reports. I knew my new openness was making a difference after a particular one-on-one conversation with a team member one day.

"Can I show you something?" he asked.

"Of course," I responded.

"This photo is of my son's hockey team. They won the state championship this weekend. I'm the coach!"

"Congratulations! I'm proud of you, Sam," I exclaimed.

I was humbled he wanted to share his proud moment with me. I was making connections.

Over the next few months, sharing more about myself started to become more natural for me, and my team excelled as individuals and collectively. I had always tried to keep my personal and professional lives separate, but showing up as a real person allowed me to be a better leader. I could have better conversations because my team knew I truly cared about them. I hadn't made the connection that this was vulnerability, but that's exactly what it was. Slowing down to get to know people allows you to better serve them and is critical to giving them your best.

The term *leader* is often used about a person in power, but usually people need a reason to follow the leader in order for the dynamic to be most effective. There needs to be a point of personal connection. A shared belief, experience, or goal. And confidence the leader has the ability and desire to support those connections. It's obvious when you look at this on a global scale. World leaders with happy and productive citizens have enabled this culture through their connection with the people. The people are willing to work in support of the leader's agenda. Leaders who don't have this connection lead through control and chaos. It's the same in our organizations, volunteer groups, and families. And the closer we work with our teams, the more personal the connection generally needs to be. Make a connection, and you will earn trust, grace, and favor. And you might gain an army.

CHINESE

WHEN OUR FAMILY HAS CHINESE TAKEOUT, we usually argue about how many servings of sesame chicken to order. I was surprised when the boys did not select sesame chicken for Chinese night. Maybe they didn't want to butcher their favorite dish. Instead, they made orange chicken and beef lo mein with some not-from-scratch pot stickers. It was the one night they were both at the stove, side-by-side, cooking it all up, laughing together. It was as if they were in a show.

Sizzle. Sizzle. "Frying the chicken is harder than I thought. There is oil everywhere!" Colten exclaimed. "Since we're cooking, I guess you get to clean it up," he said to me with a smirk.

"How different is this dish from sesame chicken?" I asked.

"Not much," Colten responded. "Mostly the sauce."

"I'm waiting for you to flip some chicken in the air," I teased. Jeremy then grabbed his wooden spoon from his wok and noodles and flung it up in a spin. He caught it against his chest. Colten flipped his spatula, and it bounced across the counter.

"Nice! You might need a little more practice before you apply at Benihana," I joked.

"Do you think they teach you how to flip things, or do you need to audition for the job?" Jeremy asked.

"Good question. Maybe you should apply and find out," I challenged.

Both dishes were great, and you could see the pride in their faces. Jeremy, who never says much at dinner, commented how well the beef lo mein turned out. I think he surprised himself.

Every Thursday, I used to ask the week's lead what we were having for dinner the next day.

"I don't know," was the typical response.

"OK, so when do you think you'll know?" I would retort. "We don't want to be rushed with grocery shopping, and we don't want to eat too late, like Polish night."

Eye rolling and groaning usually followed. "Ooookaaaaayyyy!" Although the annoyance was less obvious from John and Mom.

When I came up with the brilliant idea to make theme dinners as a family, I had it all laid out in my head. Everyone would be eager to cook as a diversion to everything else going on, which wasn't much. Remote learning at school and club soccer and social events canceled for everyone, no meet ups with friends. Everyone would look forward to it and be eager to jump in. It didn't turn out that way in practice. Although we always ended up enjoying ourselves when all was said and done.

As the weeks passed and I became less concerned about what we were actually doing and when, we all enjoyed ourselves more. I started to offer suggestions and ask how I could help and let go of the need for structure. I began to feel the difference during Chinese night as I started redirecting less and accommodating more. The actual meal wasn't the important part anyway. It was simply an excuse to be together.

Dressing the Table

Trying to get reacquainted with my kids as teenagers was certainly a tall proposition. I remember asserting my independence and sharing less with my parents during that time in my life. There was freedom, and there was frustration. I can't say my middle and high school years were radically different from anyone else's. I was a good student with a handful of close friends. I tested my boundaries, had my share of drama, and made some incredible memories. I started working at age sixteen to pay for a trip to Europe and then to buy a car. I didn't make enough for either, but because of my dedication to the causes, my parents covered the balance. In my senior year of high school, I sold a silly amount of men's sweaters over Christmas. This prompted the store manager to ask me to be assistant manager of the store instead of going to college. I declined.

I started out as a chemistry major, but then realized I was more interested in business. My school did not offer a business degree, and I didn't want to be difficult. I changed my major to psychology. This focus ended up proving much more beneficial in a business setting than I ever expected. I graduated in four years with a psychology degree and an economics minor. I was supposed to have a Spanish minor also, but found out right before graduation that credits from my semester study abroad weren't eligible. I still count it.

I worked for almost all my college career, but struggled to land my dream job, starting with my move to Spain. The friends I spent the most time with after graduation found lucrative positions in their fields or went to grad school, and I was still looking for what made me happy. I did work a high-energy office job for two years before I was laid off and then was stuck temping. I tried to keep up with my friends, but didn't feel like I was enough. My experience wasn't getting me anywhere. I knew I could be great if I was given the chance.

One day at the gym, a guy who I'd seen around town was riding a bike next to me and struck up a conversation. He told me his friend had convinced him to move to Chicago. I think he was actually hitting on me, but that conversation planted a seed. While I loved living near the beach, I needed a fresh start. I had always wanted a place with actual seasons and wanted to experience city life. NYU was my first choice of universities. I knew one person who'd moved to Chicago a few months prior, but hadn't kept in touch. I reached out to her, and we decided to be roommates. She flew out a few weeks later, and we drove everything we could fit into her car out to Chicago together. It was November.

I didn't have a job waiting for me in Chicago. But I didn't have one in San Diego, either.

I never dwelled on the possibility I might not be successful. I think I was afraid to let myself think about it. This was the second time I had moved to a new city with zero close friends and no family. And the friend I moved to Chicago with, met someone when she went home for Thanksgiving and was engaged by Christmas and living in Baltimore. Fortunately, she did introduce me to a few people before she left town who became my close friends.

After what I saw as a failed move to Spain, I was determined to make this one work. The first year was tough, but I learned a lot about myself. Like the fact I wasn't afraid to talk a big game because I had the confidence that I would figure it out. The confidence of a Southern California girl who moved to Chicago without a job as winter was settling in. I lost count of how many people looked at me cross-eyed when I told them.

This was when I was done accepting what was given to me and started treating myself as the rock star I knew I could be—although I wasn't certain what genre of music I was supposed to be playing. This was also when I learned the value in asking questions.

As I charted my own course, I felt frustrated. In a new city, with new friends and new perspectives, I realized I needed to be my own cheerleader. I began to realize that the title of a job wasn't important—it was the transferability of skills that I needed to talk about in order to get my chance. To understand this better, I became more inquisitive. I was hungry for information. Why this, not that? Why her, not him? Why here, not there? What does that mean? And one of my favorites, although not a question: Tell me more. I learned most people love to talk if you ask the right questions. They especially love to talk about themselves.

All it took was my first position as a project coordinator/office manager to see my own potential. I stopped avoiding conflict and started standing up for myself and what I knew I could achieve.

I worked for a woman with two other employees in a small graphic design office downtown. From what I saw, we didn't have a lot of work, and I certainly didn't have forty hours to do, but my boss kept busy, always rushing in and out of the office. I wasn't given much information about the projects she was working on but helped as a project admin, doing miscellaneous tasks around the office, some of which felt like busywork. I took it on myself to streamline tasks and make her more organized, which helped slow down her pace. I realized I had a gift of seeing the opportunities to make our work life better. By not being the expert, I could be the naive inquisitor, who kept people from being defensive but made them think. I helped them inspect the way they had always worked with a simple question.

"Donna, I see we're sending artwork for printing twice during most projects. Do the clients ask for that?" I asked.

"No. I'm trying to get ahead and keep the projects moving. The clients appreciate the professional print job, and it makes us look good," Donna responded.

"OK. I see that step introduces a delay while we wait for it to come back and then send it to the client. In most cases, the client has changes, and we need to go through that step again," I observed.

"That's true. But that's the way it is," she stated.

"What if we send the client a rough electronic version for their feedback before we send it out for printing? That way, we save a day and the cost of an extra print job and still get the client's feedback." This was back in the mid-1990s when email was still a new business tool and printing documents to mail or courier was the norm. Then, email systems would reject attachments much larger than 1MB. A reduction in file sizes and more consistent use of email were starting to make my recommended approach possible.

Donna stopped and stared at me, thinking. "I'm not good at email. I'm a designer."

"Understood. Could Joe send the files to the client on your behalf as your assistant?" She liked to look and feel important.

"I like that. Let's try it with the next project." Donna was on board.

With the Chinese dinner, the dish selection was completely up to the boys. They weren't ready to challenge their favorite meal, sesame chicken, but probed by trying something similar, stretched themselves, and were surprised how well the meal turned out. Well enough to get a little flashy.

Asian Orange Chicken

Yield: 4 servings
Submitted by Harry Wetzel on allrecipes.com

Ingredients

Sauce:

- 1 1/2 cups water
- 2 tablespoons orange juice
- 1/4 cup lemon juice
- 1/3 cup rice vinegar
- 2 1/2 tablespoons soy sauce
- 1 tablespoon grated orange zest
- 1 cup packed brown sugar
- 1/2 teaspoon minced fresh ginger root
- 1/2 teaspoon minced garlic
- 2 tablespoons chopped green onion
- 1/4 teaspoon red pepper flakes
- 3 tablespoons cornstarch
- 2 tablespoons water

Chicken:

- 2 boneless, skinless chicken breasts, cut into 1/2 inch pieces
- 1 cup all-purpose flour
- 1/4 teaspoon salt

- 1/4 teaspoon pepper
- 3 tablespoons olive oil

Directions

Step 1 Pour 1 1/2 cups water, orange juice, lemon juice, rice vinegar, and soy sauce into a saucepan and set over medium-high heat. Stir in the orange zest, brown sugar, ginger, garlic, chopped onion, and red pepper flakes. Bring to a boil. Remove from heat, and cool 10 to 15 minutes.

Step 2 Place the chicken pieces into a resealable plastic bag. When contents of saucepan have cooled, pour 1 cup of sauce into bag. Reserve the remaining sauce. Seal the bag and refrigerate for at least 2 hours.

Step 3 In another resealable plastic bag, mix the flour, salt, and pepper. Add the marinated chicken pieces, seal the bag, and shake to coat.

Step 4 Heat the olive oil in a large skillet over medium heat. Place chicken into the skillet and brown on both sides. Drain on a plate lined with paper towels, and cover with aluminum foil to keep warm.

Step 5 Wipe out the skillet and add the reserved sauce. Bring to a boil over medium-high heat. Mix together the cornstarch and 2 tablespoons of water; stir into the sauce. Reduce heat to medium low, add the chicken pieces, and simmer, about 5 minutes, stirring occasionally. Chicken should be cooked through.

Step 6 Serve over warm rice.

Green Tea

Have you ever been to a networking event? Many business professionals struggle to master them in order to get the most value from those events for two reasons. First, they're trying to sell people their stuff before they know if there is a need for it. Second, they aren't building relationships by understanding who they're talking with and what's important to them. This makes conversations incredibly awkward. Does this sound familiar?

"Hi, I'm Diane."

"Hi, Diane. I'm Joe."

"Nice to meet you, Joe. What do you do?"

"I own a painting company. We paint home exteriors."

"Oh, great. How long have you been doing that?"

"Twelve years."

"Longevity. That's great!"

"What do you do, Diane?"

"I'm a realtor. Here are a few of my cards. If any of your painting clients are looking to sell their home, please pass these along."

"Oh, sure."

Awkward silence.

"Nice meeting you, Diane. I'm going to grab some food before it's all gone."

If instead, you approach the event as if you truly want to know about the people you are talking with, the conversation will be much more natural. Networking is about getting to know people. This allows you to best serve them and their clientele and understand whether or not they can be of service to you and/or your customers. Again, this is all about asking questions. People love to talk about themselves. It's what they know best.

In the networking example, you probably want to walk away knowing the following:

- What product or service do they offer?
- Why are they offering it?
- Who is their ideal customer?
- What experiences brought them to this point?
- What can you do for them?
- What do they do for fun?

And if you're good, you'll engrain their name in your brain and greet them with it the next time you see them. This is a pro tip from my husband. They will be impressed, especially since they likely won't remember *your* name. Did you notice I didn't say anything about the other individual knowing all about you? Chances are, they will ask. But more importantly, you made them feel important and interesting. They will remember the way you made them feel, although they may not remember your name. This applies to all encounters. Be more curious to know how you can serve others than what you can get from them. This is the concept of Givers Gain. If you haven't read the book *The Go-Giver* by Bob Burg and John David Mann, check it out.

As I became more inquisitive, my career started to take off. I listened, learned, applied, and listened some more. Asking questions allowed me to uncover where my skills could make the biggest difference to an individual or a company. Whether the individual asked for help or not, demonstrating my value where it was needed built integrity and trust. I wasn't going back to the individual to point out how great I was, but they could see how I made their life better.

IRISH

AFTER A COUPLE OF WEEKS of the unfamiliar, we went
back to the well known. We had all traveled to Ireland for my
cousin's wedding eight years prior, and we knew what to expect.
Colten was in charge of the menu. I was almost certain one of
the items wasn't actually from Ireland, but I chose not to say
anything or look it up. The boy was happy to make fish and chips
and questioning the origin wouldn't have made a difference in
our time together. You can order fish and chips in Ireland. That
was enough.

I was proud of myself for letting it go. As I focused on being
more intentional with my thoughts and actions, I'd been consum-
ing as much information as I could about being mindful and
showing up as my best self. A coach I'd worked with frequently
talked about a quote attributed to Gerald G. Jampolsky, "You can

be right or you can be happy." I had never thought about those two options as exclusive, but in many situations they are.

From the dinners discussions it might be clear that my mom lives with us. After my father passed away, Mom didn't like what downsizing meant and became our roommate. She is incredibly independent, healthy, and has a lot of friends. It was more a move of convenience than need. She has her own kitchen and living area, and prior to the pandemic, we would typically eat together three nights a week. I started to notice interactions at dinner were focused on being right. I was focused on demonstrating I already knew what she had learned during the day and was sharing with us. I was focused on being strong and making it clear I didn't need my mom. None of it was intentional, but looking back, I saw it. My husband saw it. I was focused on having the upper hand when it didn't matter at all, at the expense of my relationship with my mom.

Mom reads the local newspaper and watches the news daily. She regularly brings us articles and tidbits of information she thinks we would be interested in, often during dinner.

"I read in the paper today that bus service won't be running for the Bolder Boulder in May. They're expecting a lot of people not to run in it because of the traffic," Mom informed us. The Bolder Boulder is an annual 10k race run on Memorial Day, which attracts over 40,000 runners. It coincides with the annual Boulder Creek Festival, and both normally bring crowds to the city.

"They're having trouble getting drivers to work the race," she added. "Maybe we should avoid going into Boulder that day."

"Well, it's still in the proposal stage. They haven't made any decisions yet," I retorted in an unfriendly tone.

"Are you sure? The article sounded a little more certain than that," she responded.

I continued, "The issue is that the Transit Department has been having trouble staffing their routes, in general, and drivers are being forced to work overtime consistently. The proposal is to cut several event-based routes, like for the Broncos and Rockies games, too." I don't usually follow the news, but I happened to have heard this story.

"Hhmmmph. Alright," she mumbled.

"We generally avoid Boulder on race day anyway because of the crowds. I hate getting stuck in traffic or having to park far away when we only live fifteen miles away," I added.

"OK," she quietly said as she focused on her plate.

I always felt bad as soon as I took the conversation in this direction.

Unfortunately, I'm not the only one who is focused on being right. Being right has become the goal. We won't listen to someone else's opinion unless it's the same as ours. We've all seen battles on social media and news threads where no one will be swayed, but everyone is ready to denounce what everyone else stands for. There is definitely a time and a place for debate and open discussion, but it only works if the people discussing are actually open to listening. As a recovering know-it-all, I was always about being right. And it cost me relationships. I thought if I was right, then I won. In reality, I lost big time.

As I shifted my career path, I looked for more opportunities to connect with my family. Not only because we couldn't go anywhere, but because I was better able to prioritize my time. I started building deeper relationships and focusing on being happy. Being more aware throughout my days of what I was doing and why, and deciding if it would result in more happiness. Happiness for my family and me. I started worrying less about being right and more about being present. Present in the moment, to enjoy the people I love the most. Now when I think about the question, *would I rather be right or be happy?* I choose happy every time. It requires intention to decide how you want to feel rather than react to your environment in the moment. It is a choice.

Mom's choice of Smithwick's and Guinness with dinner was perfect. It complemented the fish and chips, Irish stew, and apple cake well.

Buying In

As recovering vegetarians, the boys couldn't get enough beef. While I don't typically choose red meat, I didn't discourage them from making recipes including it, and I sampled it all. I didn't want to put too much structure around these nights and I wanted them to know I appreciated their effort and wanted to be inclusive. The most important thing was time with my boys. My only request was there be another main option which didn't include red meat. I think I had more beef over the three months of theme dinners than in the previous ten years.

In this case, there was beef in the Irish stew. That's also where all the vegetables were, not counting the chips, which I don't. When we first started on our healthy eating journey, I forced everyone to make a hard shift. I didn't run options by John or the kids, but demanded we all adjust. The kids were two and five, and they pushed back. Like taking away dairy in favor of non-dairy milk. This was our biggest battle. I remember nights of begging them to drink their milk as they remained at the dinner table after John and I were done. But it wasn't "milk," was their argument. I was trying to force everyone to do what I thought was right. I was the mom! It wore everyone down, including me.

My failure in this endeavor was I didn't talk to anyone first. I didn't solicit input on what would work for them. I didn't ask John what he was willing to do. I knew trying to cater to differing diets would be challenging, and I felt it was my responsibility to do what I thought was best for my family. I've since learned getting buy-in is key. Asking others who are invested in the decision what they think, and crafting the plan together, makes a significant difference. It tells the other interested parties their input and perspective matter. No one likes being forced to change. Even when their voices are little.

Over time, we settled on a more reasonable diet for everyone. A balance toward healthy choices, with deviations from time to time. The Irish stew diet—we don't all have to love each individual element, but we can appreciate they can all go together. Everyone gets to be happy, and no one cares who's right.

This flexibility has freed me from being the gatekeeper. From feeling left out when the rest of the family was scheming in secret for treats, not on my approved list. From stifling creativity and stealing joy as I was always saying "No." From feeling unappreciated for trying to take the best care of my family I could. I guided them, but they needed to make choices to best serve themselves. With teenagers, this is sometimes hard to watch. While our diet isn't perfect, it could definitely be much, much worse.

The apple cake was new to us, but dessert was never turned down in our family. Everyone has something they will never say no to. For me, it's a hug from a good friend, a date with my husband, and a meal made with my kids. Beef and all.

Irish Beef Stew

Yield: 4 to 6 servings

Fidel Murphy's Irish Pub as featured on epicurious.com

Can be prepared up to two days ahead. After preparing. cool slightly. Refrigerate uncovered until cold, then cover and refrigerate. Bring to simmer before serving.

Ingredients

- 1/4 cup vegetable oil
- 1 1/4 pounds stew beef, cut into 1-inch pieces
- 6 large garlic cloves, minced
- 8 cups beef stock or canned beef broth
- 2 tablespoons tomato paste
- 1 tablespoon sugar
- 1 tablespoon dried thyme
- 1 tablespoon Worcestershire sauce
- 2 bay leaves
- 2 tablespoons (1/4 stick) butter
- 3 pounds russet potatoes, peeled, cut into 1/2-inch pieces (about 7 cups)
- 1 large onion, chopped
- 2 cups 1/2-inch pieces peeled carrots
- 2 tablespoons chopped fresh parsley

Directions

Step 1 Heat oil in large, heavy pot over medium-high heat. Add beef and sauté until brown on all sides, about 5 minutes.

Step 2 Add garlic and sauté 1 minute. Add beef stock, tomato paste, sugar, thyme, Worcestershire sauce and bay leaves. Stir to combine. Bring mixture to boil. Reduce heat to medium-low, then cover and simmer 1 hour, stirring occasionally.

Step 3 Meanwhile, melt butter in another large pot over medium heat. Add potatoes, onion and carrots. Sauté vegetables until golden, about 20 minutes.

Step 4 Add vegetables to beef stew. Simmer uncovered until vegetables and beef are very tender, another 40 minutes. Discard bay leaves. Tilt pan and spoon off fat.

Step 5 Transfer stew to serving bowl. Sprinkle with parsley and serve.

Water Crackers

As part of my educational journey in health and wellness, I joined a community focused on inspiring healthy living. The participants came from diverse backgrounds, and everyone wanted to make a difference. The positivity and love for each other was incredible. This group became an extended family. I called it my *Happy Place*. As I grew in this community and practiced being more open, the results showed up l in my corporate career. I enjoyed the deeper relationships I had with my employees and coworkers and felt proud of what we were accomplishing. But it wasn't the same as in my *Happy Place*. This was when I started to seriously consider a career change.

It's also when I began to embrace a practice of being present. Appreciating the here and now, and not always looking for joy down the road. This practice has enabled me to better connect with the people who mean the most to me. Of course, we look at what needs to be accomplished in order to grow, but love ourselves where we are today. I encourage you to celebrate how far you've come, no matter how close you are to your destination. The small wins add up to a life of abundance.

I know being present can be difficult, especially with smartphones sending us incessant notifications and taking us away from anything we might be focused on. With a business built on social media, those bips and beeps represent business traction and growth . . . What I've learned is by compartmentalizing the notifications, I'm more productive.

Instead of being interrupted every ten minutes, I turned off my notifications and schedule times in the day to check them. It was tough for me at first, but when I did, I became exceptionally more productive and present in what I was doing. I learned to prioritize the notifications into buckets of time, allowing me to enjoy my family more, my business more, and to have more time for myself.

Meditation is another practice that has helped me be more present. By focusing on your breath and acknowledging and pushing away distractions, you are training your mind to tune out ancillary thoughts and actions. In my corporate days, I didn't think I had time for meditation. It was another thing I had to schedule into my day. I now realize it would have not only created time but helped me manage the stress in a more effective and calming way. You don't need hours. You can start with five to ten minutes.

I heard a story shortly before I resigned from my corporate job that says it all. I don't recall the source, but the message is powerful.

A man worked long hours every week. He traveled half the time and, when he was in town, was frequently found in his home office working after business hours. The man had a seven-year-old son. The boy craved time with his dad and one evening asked if his dad would play catch with him.

"I can't, son. I need to get this work done," his dad replied.

The boy sulked out of the office. He asked his dad the same question every day for a week and got the same response. On the fifth day, the boy asked his dad how much money he made.

"Why would you ask that question?" he inquired.

"You must be important. I was wondering how much your time is worth," the boy responded.

"A hundred dollars an hour," his dad replied.

The boy left with his head hung down.

The next week, the boy came back into his dad's office.

"Dad, can I borrow $100?" the boy asked.

"What do you need $100 for? I work hard for my money, and we can't just throw it away on silly toys," he barked.

"I wanted to use it to buy an hour of your time, Daddy," the boy replied.

The man sighed and started to cry, realizing what he had been putting off all this time.

It's hard for me to get through the story without my eyes welling up. I was the man.

SWEDEN

CUE "DANCING QUEEN." You know the song. We had ABBA music blaring, and were singing and dancing in the kitchen—or, mostly I was—with meatballs simmering and pancakes browning on the stove. Our trip around the world had taken us east and slightly north to Sweden.

Onion boy, Jeremy, was back in business making the Swedish meatballs. He was in charge of this week's food and picked the most involved component. He did finally come up with a solution to his onion eyes. In previous weeks, he'd tried my mom's onion goggles, but they were too small and didn't keep his eyes from watering. This week he found a snorkeling mask he started wearing every time he cut onions. It gives everyone a chuckle and works great! I tried to share the running water tip to minimize the tears, but he wasn't interested.

"The mask works fine. I don't care if the rest of you cry." That was Jeremy. Always black and white.

Jeremy has always been a creative problem solver. When we moved into a house with a vaulted ceiling in the living room, we bought a fifteen-foot Christmas tree. The challenge was decorating the top part of the tree. We used a ladder, but then only one person at a time could decorate. We also had a loft that extended over a portion of the living room. Jeremy found one of those gripper grabber claws to hang ornaments from the loft. I also caught him throwing a few onto the top. It worked.

It's an Experience

IKEA is a well-known Swedish store in the US. If you haven't been, it's a huge, two-story box selling products from Sweden. You start upstairs and are routed through the store in a predetermined way, snaking through kitchens, bedrooms, bathrooms, theater rooms, and the like. Though you generally go to IKEA for a particular reason, most people usually follow the scripted course, wandering through to get ideas or check out what's new. They are experiencing the store as a journey to the checkout line. While your initial goal in going to IKEA may have been to buy a dresser for your daughter, you may stop and pick up some new plates and a rug for your bathroom. It's part of the experience. Alternatively, you can try to shortcut the course and go directly to the dresser, but this often leads to swimming upstream, as people traffic is routed in one direction. I know this from experience.

In my technology career, I picked up a skill set in Scrum. I worked in this methodology for several years and, towards the end, became a Scrum coach. When I started out as a Scrum Master, I experimented with portions of Scrum at home. The concept with Scrum is to start with an idea of the value you want to deliver or achieve, and make progress incrementally. In the software space, this means if you're going to build a new software feature, you build the smallest component of the feature from the user interface all the way to storing data in the database and make sure it fully works before you add anything new. And, you make the status of the development visible at all times. Software development historically has required a lengthy requirements document, a development cycle of several months to several years, followed by testing. While you may have a plan outlining how long each of these activities should take, you never have a true status until you bring all the pieces together during testing.

There are several benefits to working in a Scrum model. First, finding an issue with a new feature after a couple of days of work is much simpler and less expensive than if you bring it together to test functionality after two months of work. With the latter, there are many more areas where the issue could have been introduced, and the developer has generally moved onto the next problem, taking much longer to troubleshoot and resolve.

Second, making the status visible helps you to see where there may be stalls in the execution and allows you to dig in sooner than if you take everyone's word for it. Additionally, if you decide only

70 percent of your original plan is good enough, or if the market changes and your solution will no longer bring the anticipated value, you can easily stop, thereby reducing your expense, and pivot onto the next priority.

Let me provide a more relatable example. You decide you need a completely different look, and you make an appointment at a hair salon.

"What are we doing today?" the stylist inquires.

"I want to change up my look," you respond.

"Are you thinking a new color, a new style, a new length?" she questions.

"All of those are on the table. And maybe some bangs. I brought in a picture to get us started," you say as you hand her a photo torn from a magazine.

She then proceeds to ask about various options and is ready to get started. You notice there are no mirrors on the wall but don't think much of it. She colors, cuts, and styles. Then when she's finished, she hands you a mirror.

"Uh, wow!" you say.

"Don't you love it?!" she exclaims.

"Hhhmmm," you mumble as you take the mirror and inspect your new look.

The cut is close to the picture, but way too short for your liking. And the color is not at all what you were thinking. Your appointment time is up. You have to pay and leave, and do everything you can to keep from screaming.

Now, imagine the appointment went like this.

There is a mirror on the wall in front of you, and you get to see the progress all along the way. The stylist mixes the color and tries it on a portion of your hair. After time for it to set, she rinses, and you see the color is a little lighter than you wanted. Using your feedback, she mixes again to darken it up and then applies it to your full head.

When she starts to cut, she starts with the length first. She measures with her finger to show you and then cuts when you're happy. You decide it's short enough for now.

Then she moves onto the overall style and makes some adjustments based on your reactions. You like what you're seeing and decided to hold off on the bangs for now. After she dries and styles your hair, you ask for a few minor adjustments before you decide it's enough.

In this familiar example, the stylist worked incrementally and got your feedback along the way. This included taking a second try on the color, starting with a minor length reduction, and then deciding you'd had enough change and didn't want bangs after all.

Instead of waiting for the whole style to come together at the end, you adjusted as the stylist worked. This is the core value proposition of Scrum. Try, learn, and re-prioritize. And by making everything visible as you go, you can better understand how each part integrates, and it impacts the larger whole.

Why would I use this model with my kids, you ask? Transparency and accountability. I am a recovering control freak. We had a whiteboard, which included everyone's chores and homework for the week, even the tasks John and I were working on around the house. When someone started an item, they moved the appropriate magnet to the Started column. When they were done, they moved the magnet to the Done column. When John or I inspected the work and agreed the chore was done, we moved the magnet to the Accepted column. We walked through the whiteboard most nights for about ten minutes.

The nightly gathering provided a regular reminder for the boys to keep on top of their tasks and homework without a constant nagging. Examples of items on the whiteboard were, pick up your room, brush your teeth, read for ten minutes, take a bath and update math log. The nightly meeting became an opportunity for the boys to claim success and a time for us to say, "Hey, that thing you were going to do doesn't need to be done this week because . . ." My favorite was celebrating each completed item as a win. We celebrated the small stuff as often as possible. It pumped the kids up and made them want to show up prepared. Of course, we talked about what wasn't getting done and what help they needed to move forward, but the Wins were the real focus.

We all need to celebrate wins. Being excited that you aren't crying over onions is one way, but a physical act of celebration resonates the most. A fist pump, high five, or dancing are good options. I danced while making dinner to celebrate uninterrupted time with the boys.

However, we often focus on what we're not doing or what isn't working instead of the real progress we're making. We generally don't mention our progress to our colleagues, family members, or ourselves at all. We see it as expected and not worth mentioning.

Instead, we focus on the exceptions and beat ourselves up about them. Setbacks and failure are lessons on your way to success. Do you know anyone who never made a mistake in their life and has massive success? No, you don't. People who don't make mistakes are people who are afraid to try. It's no surprise one of the core tenets of Scrum is to embrace failure. You won't always get it right, but the more you try, fail, learn, and adjust, the closer you will get to your destination. Do you think the stylist was offended when you asked her to adjust the color? Of course, not. Refinement is part of the process to get to your vision.

Taking the first step is worth celebrating. Getting it wrong but learning from the mistake and trying again is worth celebrating. Mistakes and failure are all part of the learning process. Assess, adjust, and keep going. Success isn't only about reaching the end, but the journey that got you there. Like the IKEA experience, the lessons build on one another. Trying to jump ahead generally leads to frustration and backtracking. Acknowledge how much you've grown and use the growth as motivation to keep going.

If you've ever been a bystander in a marathon, you should understand the concept of regular celebration. All along the race route, spectators are cheering and screaming the runners on, celebrating how far they've come as each step gets them closer to the finish line. I encourage you to look at your own actions and celebrate how each is moving you towards your vision.

As noted previously, when our family cooks, onions are hard to avoid. At first, Jeremy wanted to steer clear of them. He asked for other tasks. When he was in charge of Swedish night and picked meatballs as the main component, he faced the obstacle and took the first step towards a solution with the onion goggles. When those weren't adequate, he found a swim mask. He didn't need to waste time on another solution as the one he had was good enough. Jeremy solved his onion problem and didn't need to consider the running water idea. He is never one to waste an ounce of energy. Good enough is good enough for him. Jeremy celebrated with dry eyes. The rest of us celebrated his ingenuity by capturing it on camera.

Swedish Meatballs

Yield: 6 servings
From damndelicious.net

Ingredients

Meatballs:

- 2 tablespoons olive oil, divided
- 1 onion, diced
- 1 pound ground beef
- 1 pound ground pork
- 1/2 cup Panko (Japanese style breadcrumb)
- 2 large egg yolks
- 1/4 teaspoon ground allspice
- 1/4 teaspoon ground nutmeg
- Kosher salt and freshly ground black pepper, to taste

Gravy:

- 1/4 cup unsalted butter
- 1/3 cup all-purpose flour
- 4 cups beef broth
- 3/4 cup sour cream
- Kosher salt and freshly ground black pepper, to taste
- 2 tablespoons chopped fresh parsley leaves

Directions

Step 1 Heat 1 tablespoon olive oil in a large skillet over medium heat. Add onion, and cook, stirring frequently, until onions have become translucent, about 2–3 minutes.

Step 2 In a large bowl, combine ground beef, ground pork, Panko, egg yolks, allspice, nutmeg, and cooked onion; season with salt and pepper, to taste. Using a wooden spoon or clean hands, stir until well combined. Roll the mixture into 1 1/4-to-1 1/2-inch meatballs, forming about 24 meatballs.

Step 3 Add remaining 1 tablespoon olive oil to the skillet. Add meatballs, in batches, and cook until all sides are browned, about 4–5 minutes. Transfer to a paper towel-lined plate.

Step 4 To make the gravy, melt butter in the skillet. Whisk in flour until lightly browned, about 1 minute. Gradually whisk in beef broth and cook, whisking constantly, until slightly thickened, about 1–2 minutes. Stir in sour cream; season with salt and pepper, to taste.

Step 5 Stir in meatballs and cook, stirring occasionally, until heated through and thickened, about 8–10 minutes.

Step 6 Serve immediately, garnished with parsley, if desired.

Sorbet

Ask anyone what their dream vacation, dream job, dream anything is, and they can generally give you an idea without much thought. Usually those dreams are on a five- to ten-year or more horizon. Far enough into the future, most people don't have a clue how to get there. If I asked what your life will be like in four years, how many people would be able to answer with any amount of confidence? Virtually zero, because it's more difficult to plan the farther out a target is.

But most of us have these amazing dreams, with our only plan being hope. Our linear thinking makes it difficult to come up with the steps to get us that far down the road, and we struggle to start. A large task can be daunting.

What if, like Scrum, we plan in two-week increments, or even less? Set a goal for what you want to accomplish at the end of two weeks and work towards it. Measure anything you are considering doing against the two-week goal. If the new activity enables your goal, go for it! If the new activity detracts from your goal, don't do it. If the new activity is neutral, determine if it's still worthwhile before jumping in. Sometimes a distraction is needed as long as it doesn't take you too far off course. But remember, the goal is not finite, but a direction. If the goal is no longer serving you, change it.

At the end of the two weeks, celebrate what you accomplished and then reevaluate if the tasks you didn't complete are still taking you in the right direction and if they're still at the top of the priority list.

Say you want to move to Italy within three years and travel around Europe. You don't know Italian and don't work for a company with offices there. Also, you're not sure exactly where you want to live. Your list of prioritized to-dos might look like the one below, with the first block of items planned into the next couple of weeks.

Block 1: Research options to learn Italian and make a list of topics you are passionate about.

To Dos:

- Pick a target date for moving
- Select a language course and enroll
- Evaluate your list of passions for opportunities to make income
- Complete X amount of the language course
- Research areas of Italy you might want to live and put them into a loose prioritized list
- Map your income opportunities against locations to understand which are most viable
- Complete Y of the language course

When you get to the end of block 1, celebrate what you completed, confirm your prioritized list of to dos, and select items for block 2. With this approach, after eight weeks, you'd be well on your way to making a move to Italy a reality, compared to the hope most people throw at their dreams.

For our dinners, the goal was deliberate family time. We planned each week one week out, and when the fun waned after thirteen weeks, we let it go. The goal was achieved. Each dinner was our celebration.

THAI

ALMOST THREE MONTHS INTO OUR theme dinners, we were starting to get a little burned out. We'd planned on Indian food, but no one wanted to take the lead. John and I had traveled to Thailand a few years prior and were impressed with the street food. The exchange student we sponsored a year later confirmed that many Thai families eat their meals from the street markets most nights. While we had taken cooking lessons in Thailand and included Thai in our regular meal rotation, this week, we decided to stick with the Thai norm and opted for takeout. We still got to spend time together, but less in the kitchen and more playing Dungeons and Dragons (D&D) with Jeremy as the Dragon Master.

For anyone who may have been watching us, we were certainly a motley cast of characters. If you're not familiar with D&D, each person takes on a persona, and then the group travels on a quest of some sort, battling villains and slaying dragons and other creatures. You advance through different levels, all created by the Dragon Master, and gain possessions and skills as you go. We were a seven-foot half-elf who was a thief, a two-and-a-half-foot drunken monk, an athletic wizard, and a warrior with a German accent. We had a goal of finding out who was plotting to kill the king, but had little idea how to accomplish it.

While we were working together, there wasn't a lot of trust. The half-elf stole from all of the nuns when we stopped at a church and asked for help. The monk's favorite weapon was explosives, and given his love for the sauce, we were never sure if we should hide when he used them or trust they would hit the intended target. The wizard was the one tapped to lead the quest by the king, but struggled to conjure her spells consistently, and the warrior hadn't mastered the art of javelin throwing, although he tried to use his javelins often. Would you want this group helping you to stop a lethal attack? Fortunately, this was make-believe.

Don't Delay

It felt good to get lost in a made-up world. Make-believe wasn't something I let myself enjoy often as I became serious about my goals. Growing up, my mom had talked about me going to high school in Germany, where both her parents were from. I loved the idea and assumed it would happen one day. I had been given a Berlitz book on German, but no other guidance or direction. No one gave me a study plan or a timeline, and I didn't ask. When I inquired about studying abroad as high school got closer, my mom almost laughed at me. I felt stupid and let down. To me, it was a big deal, but I didn't do anything to make the experience a reality.

In high school, when the chance to go to Europe for a month came up, I immediately found a job to make the trip happen. When I went to college, I knew I wanted to study abroad. My school didn't have an official program, but I did my research and found a program through another university. When I went to Spain after college, I funded my way there, as well. While very driven, I was always working towards the next milestone, and often more than one.

I was ambitious, worked hard, and was always incredibly coachable. If you told me what I needed to do to move forward, I immediately prioritized the activity item into my list. I didn't wait for something to happen. I jumped in.

Our family camping trips usually included a group of family friends. I loved exploring, catching pollywogs, and playing in the dirt with the other kids. On one particular trip, when I was four, another mom walked by our campsite.

"Cheryl, the next time I see you with a clean face, I'll give you a dime," she said to me.

I jumped up and ran into our trailer. "Mommy! Mommy! Clean my face! Mrs. Jones is gonna give me a dime!"

She told me what I needed to do, and I got into action. I wasn't taking any chances I might see her again with a clean face before we all went back home. I've always had the perspective that if an outcome is important or an opportunity arises, don't sit on it. At four years old, there was nothing on my list more significant than getting a dime.

I mentioned John and I had the opportunity to travel to Thailand. He had met up with some friends from college one weekend, one of whom lives in Thailand. He told his friend we would come visit him in the next couple of years. Knowing John, it sounded to me like a good intention but would likely never happen. I suggested we start looking at dates and plans. We ended up in Thailand five months later. If you're serious about a goal, do more than dream about it. Prioritize it into your time commitments and take steps in the direction you want to go.

It's no surprise my career revolved around planning. As a program manager, it was about understanding the What, defining the How, and then crafting the When. From there, we lived by the plan until we reached the end. Of course, there were changes, but always with understanding of how change impacted the journey and the end game. The tactics and details changed when I embraced Scrum, but the general idea was still the same. Know where you want to go, take steps towards it, and learn and adjust, as needed.

The point here is I was always focused on the next big goal. Yes, I would take time to celebrate when we hit one, but then immediately focus on what's next. That's why I was good at my job. I kept everyone moving forward. The problem was I wasn't enjoying the here and now. My happiness was always somewhere down the road. Nothing going on today was good enough.

The ironic part is I've always been a bit of a risk-taker, as you've seen already. I've made three moves to a new city without a job. When my husband and I moved from Chicago to Denver, Jeremy was nine weeks old, and John had the promise of a trading opportunity. When we arrived, the company he was supposed to work with had all but folded. We both started looking for opportunities, and each found something quickly. Not our dream positions, but we were bringing in income. John's job required him to work every Saturday. While I know he didn't love this, I resented it. Instead of appreciating his diligence and focusing on what I had—alone time with my adorable young son—I focused on the fact I knew almost no one else, and I was eager to explore my new surroundings with John. Maybe it was a bit of postpartum exhaustion, but I was feeling abandoned. I knew our situation was temporary and yet could only focus on changing it. As a control freak, if situations didn't work out exactly as I had seen them in my head, I dwelled on the disconnect. I didn't make lemonade. I squirted the lemons in everyone else's eyes.

When I found a solid position, I started scrambling up the ladder quickly, focusing only on the next rung. I was afraid to be seen as a mom at the workplace, presenting a tough, dedicated leader in the technology world instead. Unfortunately, I missed out on a lot with my young kids. The boys felt it, too.

"Mom, can you come to my classroom for our Manners breakfast?" Jeremy asked when he was in second grade.

"No, I have to work," I sighed. This was well before work from home was a common option, and I could run up to the school for an hour. Instead, I would have to take a half day off from work, and I wanted to save vacation time for more extended time with the family.

"Are you coming on my field trip next week?" Colten begged.

"I can't, buddy," I sighed. "I'll try next time."

I was focused on providing the best I could for my family financially and being seen by the higher ups, to continue the cycle. I became consumed with finishing whatever project I was working on because I knew there was more right behind it. I had serious guilt and struggled with my internal conflict. I did finally make it to some of their in-class events and field trips before they were out of elementary school, but I do regret not being with them and their classmates more. It is one of the few things I would change if I could.

I am in full support of setting goals to set you in the direction of what you desire. However, we can often get laser focused on our target and forget to look up to see what's going on around us. Regular assessment and reevaluation are critical, otherwise, you can end up at your targeted destination but far from where you actually want to be. Although a simplistic example, ordering Thai takeout instead of cooking as planned allowed us to change course, and honor the intent of what I had set out to do over forcing a plan for the plan's sake. We honored time with the family and navigated the underground as a ridiculous foursome on behalf of the king. I'm not sure the monk even knew why he was there.

GIVE THANKS

WHILE ALL THE FOOD WE MADE during our quarantine dinners was incredible, my favorite night was when we made breakfast.

Typically, we'd pick the theme for the next week as we were finishing the current week's meal. "What are we having next week?" I asked.

"Breakfast!" shouted Colten, followed by snickers and sneers from the table.

"Sounds great!" I responded.

"Really?" Jeremy inquired.

"Sure. What do we want to make?" I reassured them.

The boys were completely shocked that I went for the idea. They were sure I would shoot it down. I was done controlling and was happy to enjoy whatever time together I could. The excitement shot up.

"French toast!"

"Crepes!"

"Biscuits and gravy!"

"Chocolate fountain!" Everyone burst into laughter. The fountain comes up whenever we talk about brunch.

We decided on French toast, biscuits and gravy, eggs, and sausage. Mom spoiled us with orange juice and mimosas. Since we'd made all the various components of our breakfast meal before, we knew exactly how much time each would take and didn't have to scramble for ingredients. Not only were we stuffed, but the pressure was off for everybody. As I let go, turned down the heat, and focused on the company, everyone relaxed. Breakfast for dinner. Never a bad idea.

As I look back, I am surprised at how much I learned from the thirteen weeks of theme dinners. How our once-a-week event helped me understand what was truly important to me and let go of the rest. My practice of controlling activities for the sake of achieving an ad hoc vision wasn't serving anyone. Being present, embracing the evening, and being actively grateful for what I had was more freeing and fulfilling than I had expected. And I wanted more.

When I decided to leave my technology career, I was definitely nervous, but I can't say I was afraid. It was time to prioritize my family in a more personal way and build the family dynamic I had always wanted. Although I regretted not being able to attend all the boys' activities when they were younger, my commitment to my career made the most sense at the time. And I'm at peace with that decision. When it was time, I made my move and focused on how to optimize the change for my family, but I've learned that move made a difference for many others. As Brene Brown explains, you can't have courage without vulnerability, and my choice to leave a successful corporate career was definitely courageous.

As I considered the change, I had moments of wondering, *What will people think?* But then I reflected on life being practice and a journey of learning. It's OK to change course to find the most appropriate lessons for you and your situation. When we embrace the lessons and center ourselves on what we believe in and who we are, we stop determining our self-worth based on someone else's achievements. You are the only you. Surround yourself with those who inspire and challenge you to be your best self. To be happy.

As I navigated my career transition from the corporate technology world, I implemented a more consistent and deliberate practice of gratitude. This isn't about saying "Thank you" when someone holds the door for you or sends you a gift, but setting time aside to reflect on what you are truly grateful for. As discussed earlier, we over-rotate on what's not working, what we're not happy about, who is not playing along. When we do this, our mind focuses on those negatives and brings us more. When we remind ourselves of all the good in our lives, our brain brings us more positivity.

I've implemented gratitude as a regular practice in two ways. Before I get out of bed in the morning, I think about three events from the previous day I'm grateful for. This could be my teenager hugging me without being asked, a stranger at the grocery store picking up my dropped item because she saw my hands were full, or my amazing husband cooking a gourmet meal for me. The second way is keeping a gratitude journal to write it all down. When I'm having bad days, I can go back through it to remind myself how blessed I am. Practicing gratitude before I pick up my phone in the morning helps get my mind in the right place as I kick off the day.

When practicing gratitude, the key is to identify new items every day. Your brain thrives on fresh concepts to maintain alertness for gratitude. Instead of being thankful for my incredibly supportive mom, maybe today I'm grateful she was able to make dinner for the boys, allowing John and I to have a date night. Research shows happiness is strongly tied to relationships. Focusing our gratitude on people and their actions rather than circumstances or material things heightens the experience.

I'd been sharing this notion of gratitude with John for several months and he would nod and smile. "I'm grateful," he'd say. I could tell he saw gratitude as an action rather than a state of mind. With a finance background, he saw success as numbers. He hadn't yet embraced mindset as a critical factor to happiness. John runs a nutraceutical company. In looking for new trends to bring to market, he attended a virtual conference on biohacking. Biohacking is the concept of managing one's own biology using a combination of medical, nutritional, environmental, and electronic techniques. This is the idea behind the movie and TV series *Limitless*. During the conference, there was a section on gratitude and how your thoughts determine how you feel and perform. John wasn't expecting concepts like gratitude and mindset to be discussed. But he couldn't ignore the validation. He started meditating regularly soon thereafter.

One of my business partners also attended the event and was there for all the topics John wasn't. Our business is helping women feel their best physically and mentally. I never would have expected the two of them to attend the same event unless I was in the middle of it, but this is another great example of perspective. We come into situations with different experiences, expectations, and goals. Being open and willing to listen to variations and how they can expand our understanding is powerful.

It probably comes as no surprise, but most people think way more about themselves than they do about anyone else. Yet, we're always concerned about what other people are thinking about us! The good news is, they're not. After you run into someone on the street, they have purged you from their mind and are back to thinking about themselves in about fifteen seconds. They aren't laughing at the spinach in your teeth or the stain on your shirt or disgusted by your windblown hair. They are back to thinking about numero uno, themselves. It's human nature. Of course, our loved ones get a chunk of our attention, but generally, we are inwardly focused.

Gratitude for the actions of others helps to reinforce our similarities and sends more positivity into the universe. Practicing gratitude gives you a leg up on tough days. Remembering all the good in your life can dwarf the challenges. There is no end to the number of situations, events, and interactions we can be grateful for. I bet if you think back on the last twenty-four hours, you'll have a whole list.

I'm grateful my family engaged in my crazy theme dinner idea and played along. I'm grateful a friend of my husband's suggested I write a book about our theme dinner adventures. And I'm grateful you decided to read my story.

I'm definitely a rule follower, but I'm not afraid to change up the ingredients, and see what happens next. Variations are what make life interesting. I urge you to continually measure, mix, and marinate until you get the desired result.

I leave you with what's typically the first meal of the day as the ending to my tale—the taste of French toast on your tongue, the smell of sausage in the air, and the feeling of mimosas on your brain. Cheers!

EPILOGUE: SERVE IT UP

GROWING UP, I always expected to get married and have kids. I didn't dream about my wedding or about being a mom but understood both were somewhere on the journey. I was confident in my abilities to survive and take care of myself, and I knew I wanted to have a solid career before I entertained a serious relationship after college. I was a Psychology major in a Business and Technology world. I had to prove to myself I belonged there.

I had no intention of relying on favors from family and friends, my looks, my partner's career, or anything but my own contributions. I needed to prove to myself I could support myself and didn't need anyone else to get by. I'd heard stories of too many women destitute because they couldn't stand on their own. Women who stayed in relationships because they were dependent on someone else for money or skills. Women whose only option was to serve their husband and when the relationship soured were miserable emotionally and financially. I wanted to be in control of my options.

I landed in the male-dominated technology industry. As I grew in my career, I found it harder to connect with other women, especially those without a corporate background. I saw being emotional as the quickest way to lose the respect of my peers and superiors. I was afraid to show my weak side to anyone, close friends included. I was like an actor who stayed in character on and off the set while filming a movie. I didn't share weakness, failure, silliness, or stress. I enjoyed and appreciated my friends but kept my flaws and fears locked under armor, and I didn't acknowledge them to myself. I looked ahead and kept swimming.

As the stay-at-home orders started lifting across the country, I was invited to attend a retreat with a handful of amazing women in my business. The last evening we were together, we started getting real. It was my turn.

"I've never related to women well," I confessed.

"What?" commented one of the other ladies whom I'd met that weekend. "I didn't pick up on that at all."

"I don't feel I can share myself. That I have a relatable story," I added.

"You know that's the story you're telling yourself," the retreat organizer retorted. We were all students of Brene Brown, and this is one of her teachings. We make up stories about what we think is going on with other people all the time, and they're usually not true. Brene Brown also calls this concept our "shitty first draft." We usually decide and react on a story before we confirm. When we do dig further, we usually get a better, more honest version of the story.

She went on, "I bet you there are a lot of women who feel the same way. This is your opportunity to connect with and inspire them."

I'd been hearing from many people about how I was inspiring them with my vulnerability and positivity on social media. I was connecting, but maybe not in the way I thought I should. That evening I was vulnerable and open, and got the support I needed. I knew I was in the right place.

As a mom, I knew my role was to serve and protect. To teach the boys right and wrong; to give them tools to learn and gain confidence; to feed them physically and emotionally; to be their biggest fan. Like with my career, I approached being a mom like a checklist. Get through the "have-to" stuff, and they'll know I love them. What I didn't appreciate is connection is in the ad hoc, unplanned moments. Moments with my kids, my friends, and my coworkers. By letting go of the outcome and allowing for the unstructured, opportunities to be present, to connect, and to serve appear.

My way may have been the most direct and efficient, but was it the most productive? It depends on the goal. I always looked at the goal as completing the task before me and moving onto the next one. I ignored the experience of the journey. I always thought I could reflect on the journey when I got to the destination. But instead, once I reached the checkered flag, I sped onto the next track.

If you're walking your kids home from school and you take the same direct way you have always gone, you'll probably get home the quickest. But, if you let your six-year-old pick which way to turn at each street, within reason of course, you'll likely see all new scenarios which can become points of connection.

Maybe a neighbor got a new puppy you wouldn't have known about. He is incredibly soft and jumped all over the both of you. And his puppy breath!

Perhaps your son learns four right turns take you back to where you started. How did that happen? Isn't that crazy?!

Maybe you meet a new kid who has moved into the neighborhood the same age as your daughter. A new friend! And she'll be in her class!

The checklist serves a great purpose of identifying tasks, but if you don't look up from the list, you will miss a lot. As I began working on my leadership skills, I started to be more introspective about who I could serve and who I needed to become to give others my best. I knew I needed to work on myself. And I'm certainly not done. We're all a work in progress.

As I started to be more open and vulnerable, I became more present. It wasn't about completing tasks, but about experiencing the moment. Feeling, absorbing, sharing, and connecting. About understanding how my actions impacted others and how I could help them have the best experience. How I could show up to serve them today. It goes back to the concept of Giver's Gain. If your motivation is selfish, people will see it and feel it. But if you are truly interested in their happiness and success, and not about how you benefit or you look, the universe will reward you.

In high school, my best friend and I had a bond about not being cheerleaders. We had plenty of friends who were cheerleaders; it simply wasn't our gig. I'm sure most high schoolers are more concerned about how they look to everyone else than empowering each other, but I carried the thinking with me for a while. I had to protect myself. Overtly building up others showed how they were better than I was. I needed to be strong before I could give. I had to be in control all the time. At least that's what I told myself.

Now my high school friend and I both cheer other people on for a living. Not only as moms and spouses, but as coaches and leaders in our respective organizations. It's an amazing feeling when you know you had a hand in someone else's achievement. You enabled them to see their true power. And by being in their corner, trust increases, and so does your connection. As I mentioned earlier, we tend to overlook progress as we stare at the obstacles. Almost no one makes a straight line towards their target. A sidestep is often needed to continue making progress. Sometimes we need a gentle reminder we are moving forward, and the investment in ourselves is worth it. When we can accept that every one of us has our own story, which leads to our unique perspective and opportunity to make an impact, we can begin celebrating each other's wins instead of resenting them.

As I've become more introspective, I've noticed a shift in my relationship with Mom. We live under the same roof (i.e., it's not perfect), but I am now more aware of my thoughts and actions in our interactions. I can see her intention in a clearer way and don't feel as compelled to trump her. I'm now looking for connection and opportunities to make her feel loved and appreciated.

We are on this planet to serve and support each other. Relationships are the key to surviving and thriving. When we focus on how we can serve in our daily lives, our world expands. I'm not talking about massive events or actions requiring extensive sacrifice for you, but shifting your lens. As Sarah Bernhardt stated, "Life begets life. Energy creates energy. It is only by spending oneself that one becomes rich."

When you spend your energy, consider the return on investment. Does it end with you? Or does it multiply? Who else does it serve? Rather than "What's in it for me?" contemplate "What's in it for them?" Ask yourself how you can bring value and make a difference, one small action at a time. Pay attention to the results and see the joy you create, not only for those you serve but for yourself.

FEED YOUR SOUL

AS I MENTIONED, I'm on a mission to help more women feel their best mentally and physically. As nurturers, we often put ourselves at the bottom of the list and take the leftovers rather than listening to what we need to make the biggest impact and share our gifts. If you're looking for tools to help you shift your mindset and lean into your greatness, visit me at key-ingredients. com to download my four tools for prioritizing yourself, serving at a higher level, and begin attracting what you want.

ACKNOWLEDGMENTS

I COULD NOT HAVE WRITTEN THIS BOOK without the support of my incredible husband, John. He is my biggest cheerleader and a remarkable father. When I told John I wanted to leave my successful career in technology to be more present in his and our boys' lives, he didn't blink an eye. He knew I wanted more for myself and our family, and he was willing to figure it out together.

If my sons, Jeremy and Colten, had not played along with the weekly dinner idea, this book would never have happened. Thanks, boys, for your patience with the dinners and patience with me as I navigated my career change.

Thanks to my mom for showing me what it looks like to be a working mom and also enjoy life. Our family camping adventures gave me an appreciation for the great outdoors and how life is right in front of us, not somewhere down the road. I only wish I had paid attention sooner.

I am always inspired by my dad and his demonstration that anything is possible, if you set your intention. He and his four siblings were scattered across different families and care homes at an early age as a result of alcoholism and divorce. When they were reunited, Dad fought his way back at the encouragement of his stepdad, Jerry. Despite originally having no intention of attending college, Dad graduated with a BS and then an MS in civil engineering, becoming a sought-after structural engineer, and ultimately opened up his own engineering firm as a respected community figure. Dad repeatedly paid it forward and was an incredible product of what a little encouragement and kindness can do.

Thanks to Lisa Blaisdell for setting the example and encouraging me to be more vulnerable and level up. Lisa demonstrated that being successful isn't about how much money you earn but the life you create and the impact you make.

I'd always wanted to write a book, but the inspiration for what to write never hit me. As I posted the results of our weekly dinners on social media, John's college friend, Dave Dutton, suggested I write a book about it. Thanks for the inspiration, Dave.

Thanks to all the working moms whose voices are now accounted for in the way we work, the products we make, and the corporate cultures we are creating. You are not only dedicated moms, but I see your determination and the sacrifices you make for your families and the companies who employ you. You never ask for the praise you deserve, but continue on. I encourage you to put yourself at the top of the list. I am here to cheer you on.

ABOUT THE AUTHOR

CHERYL SCHUBERTH is a graduate of the University of California San Diego and a respected corporate leader. She holds multiple coaching and leadership certifications from the Project Management  Institute, Scrum Alliance, and Brené Brown's *Dare to Lead,* and is a sought-after coach and mentor. As a wife, mom, and former corporate go-getter, Cheryl knows firsthand the frustration of trying to do it all and feeling that none of it is good enough. After twenty-five years leading and coaching teams in the male-dominated technology space, she stepped away from that world and embarked on a mission to enhance her relationships with her teenage sons and, at the same time, empower other working women to become more curious about their options and reevaluate their priorities. She now coaches women to help them feel their best, increase their confidence, and put themselves at the top of the list. Cheryl lives outside Boulder, CO, where she enjoys hiking, skiing, and all things outdoors. You can connect with her at key-ingredients.com or @cherylschuberth on Instagram.

Made in the USA
Monee, IL
09 September 2021